DAKTRONICS

AND

THE MAN WHO LIT IT UP

By
Chuck Cecil

ISBN: 978-1893490-15-4
Library of Congress Control Number: 2007925948

Printed in the United States of America
Second Printing 2013

ALLEGRA
301 Main Ave.
Brookings, SD 57006

Table of Contents

1. A Good Beginning 1

2. New Generations 11

3. Farming's Early Lessons 23

4. Daydreams and Magnetism 35

5. New Horizons 51

6. A Partnership Formed 63

7. The "Wow" Factor 77

8. Going to the Mat 101

9. Great Timing 125

10. Olympian Efforts 135

11. The New Beginning 149

12. Plowing New Ground 161

CNN Financial News Interview 171

Honors and Awards 175

Index 179

On the cover: Dr. Aelred Kurtenbach. Photo by Melby Photography.

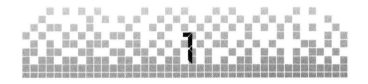

A Good Beginning

Leaning into the chill of an early-morning winter wind that whistled through New York City's concrete canyons, Dr. Aelred (Al) Kurtenbach and his wife Irene hurried from the curbside taxi to the entrance of the NASDAQ MarketSite at 43rd and Broadway. It was an important day in their lives and in the life of the company founded by the Kurtenbachs and Duane and Phyllis Sander in 1968.

That company, Daktronics, was a name Kurtenbach had dreamed up in 1968 while on a long trip to Dayton, Ohio. The idea came to him as he drove near Indianapolis. He hurriedly scribbled it out as he drove and flipped the small white piece of paper up to a bare spot on the car's dashboard where he temporarily stored his random thoughts, ideas and other "to do" notes while traveling.

Today, Daktronics, Inc., excels in the control of large display systems, including those that require integration of multiple complex displays showing real-time information, graphics, animation, and video. The company started by the Kurtenbachs and the Sanders designs, manufactures, sells, and services computer-programmable display systems, message boards, and scoreboards around the world.

On that cold December 9, 2003, an entourage of thirty Daktronics directors, employees and friends would participate in the ceremonial opening of the stock market trading day. Daktronics had been selected by NASDAQ officials to the open the market in recognition and honor of the South Dakota company's 35-year anniversary. Over those three and one-half decades, Daktronics had become a recognized worldwide leader in the design and manufacture of electronic scoreboards, large computer-programmable displays and large screen video displays utilizing light emitting diode (LED) technology. In fact, not far from the NASDAQ location, millions of those little, magical diodes were flashing Daktronics displays, adding to the excitement of bustling Times Square. The Daktronics products extolled the virtues and conveyed the corporate vitality of such well-known businesses as Morgan Stanley, Lehman Brothers, and Coca-Cola. They were just three of nine spectacular displays in that area of the Big Apple that had been designed, fabricated, and installed by Daktronics.

With the soon-to-begin daily trading, Daktronics, at that time one of only four publicly traded South Dakota firms, would be the first South Dakota company ever to be singled out for the symbolic opening of the NASDAQ market trading for the day. It would be a well-earned honor and accolade for a company that had started watch-fob small with just two employees laboring in a run-down side street building in Brookings, South Dakota, that it shared with a tire shop. The company's growth since then was the "proof in the pudding" that Kurtenbach and Sander had long espoused.

Their home state, traditionally an exporter of agricultural products as well as many of its most talented young people, had entered a new era, and Kurtenbach, Sander, and Daktronics were bellwethers in this gradual state-wide conversion from a consumer of products to a creator of product, from an exporter of youth to one determined to retain more of South Dakota's best and brightest. Kurtenbach was one of the early advocates for all this. He believed there was need for South Dakota to break out from its almost exclusive agrarian shell and to encourage other areas of creativity and manufacturing. He had long articulated the importance of developing more industry in the state, particularly in high tech niches made possible by the advances in communication, electronics and the magic of the computer. These could provide the challenges and jobs for talented young South Dakotans who would rather remain in the state but had to leave to find opportunities elsewhere. Kurtenbach contended it was an unnecessary exportation of the state's most valued resource—its young people. Again and again he used the weight of his reputation, his own experiences while he was searching for his future, and his persuasive talents to urge South Dakotans to reach out and to become bold and creative leaders in the world's expanding marketplace. When it came to highly technical industry, South Dakotans could succeed as well as any. He believed that, and he would argue that the people of the state should not stand meekly by, and looking down at their shoes.

Dr. Kurtenbach hoped his firm's NASDAQ honor and trade day visibility would be important news worldwide as well as in the little town of Dimock, South Dakota, population 180. His early interests in electronics and entrepreneurship had been ignited there in the 1940s when he was a dutiful, serious student in the Sts. Peter and Paul Catholic School. Benedictine nuns taught grades one through eight in the brick schoolhouse in the shadow of its parent church. Dimock was a little "L- shaped" wide spot in the road with good people, well-kept homes, and neatly trimmed yards, and it harbored fond memories for Kurtenbach. He felt the church, the town, and the people of Dimock, and nearby Parkston, where he attended high school, had all contributed to the influences, the wherewithal, and the philosophies that now ran deep in his psyche.

He was born in 1934 on the farm homesteaded by his paternal grandparents. The farm was within sight of Dimock and the massive Sts. Peter and Paul Catholic Church around which the little town and the larger agrarian community and neatly cared-for farms clustered. As he grew, shaped by the landscape and by that church, he watched his parents and the others in the area struggling to survive during the difficult Dust Bowl times of dirt storms, drought, and economic hard times. These horrendous conditions had upset plans and turned dreams topsy-turvy. Many who had settled there would pack up during the decade of his birth and leave for greener pastures. Life on the scorching Great Plains was further exacerbated by fluttering, gluttonous hordes of hungry grasshoppers that greedily consumed crops and anything edible, including window curtains, fence posts, and pitchfork handles permeated with the salt of hard work. It seemed to many as if the end of the world had arrived. Kurtenbach has childhood memories of those hard times that perhaps more than anything soured his father to the noble profession of farming and caused him to convince his son Aelred to find another future.

Now, years beyond that difficult decade and inside the bustling NASDAQ Media Center where more people were at work than ever lived in Dimock, Kurtenbach and Irene met and mingled with relatives, friends and other officials of the Brookings-based company as they waited for the trading day to begin. Everything had been planned down to the second by NASDAQ representatives and Kurtenbach's staff. Because there was concern for security in this city still recovering from the horrible World Trade

Center attack on Sept. 11, 2001, the party was delayed momentarily while a manifest of everyone in the party was verified and photo identifications were checked. With that preliminary completed, the South Dakota delegation was ushered into a room to await the time of the nationally televised announcement.

Company co-founder Dr. Duane Sander, who like Dr. Kurtenbach was a former electrical engineering professor at South Dakota State University in Brookings, was there with his wife, Phyllis, and the others, and with his subtle, friendly humor and wry smile, Sander greeted and spoke briefly to his colleague and longtime partner.

Arrival at the MarketSite that brisk morning was at exactly 8:50 a.m., followed by a welcome and a hurried continental breakfast. At precisely 9:12, Kurtenbach stood before the cameras for a screen check, and at 9:17 there was an on-stage run-through. Six minutes later the NASDAQ's Director of Corporate Client Group, Jack Hamilton, welcomed Kurtenbach.

On cue, at exactly 9:25 a.m., Kurtenbach was asked to make a few comments. Stepping to the dais with a slight, barely perceptible favoring of his right knee (the life-long souvenir of his childhood

Daktronics co-founder Dr. Aelred Kurtenbach opening the NASDAQ market in New York City on Dec. 9, 2003, the thirty-fifth anniversary of the founding of Daktronics.

pony's misstep into a badger hole in the pasture north of the Kurtenbach farm home) Kurtenbach made a few remarks from memory, having previously written out what he intended to say on three sheets of lined yellow paper.

He mentioned that Daktronics was a South Dakota-based technology company specializing in large, dynamic displays. He said the company was a "spin out of South Dakota State University" and that the company employed about four hundred South Dakota State University students on a part-time basis and had two hundred graduates of the university on full-time

4

status. "We provide scoreboards for all sports and venues and large, dynamic displays of all shapes to inform and entertain people," he said. He told the audience there and millions more watching on television that the company served the sport, business, and transportation markets with a "large suite of display products, control software, and service." Kurtenbach mentioned the 1,300 employees working in 370,000 square feet of space in Brookings, South Dakota. He said Daktronics had $180 million in annual sales and 7 percent net profit. He then thanked "our loyal customers, employees, and stockholders."

As planned, he completed his brief remarks at 9:28 and was then joined at the podium by the other smiling and happy Daktronics guests. With ten seconds to go before the market would be officially opened by Kurtenbach, the countdown started. Then, Kurtenbach and Daktronics made history. Trading, including for the company known by ticker tape watchers as DAKT, began.

Earlier during that visit to New York, Kurtenbach had appeared as a guest on the CNN *Financial News* with Pat Kirenan and Ali Velshi. (See interview transcript on page 171.)

Ten years earlier after a number of trips to New York, on February 10, 1994, Daktronics had announced the public offering of 1,325,000 shares of common stock at a price of $7.625 per share. Response to that offering was brisk, and an additional 183,750 shares were offered four days later. Now, after this latest CNN*fn* interview and the opening of trading, there were pictures and hugs and handshakes all around. Then the joyous Daktronics contingent left the Media Center and Kurtenbach treated everyone to a celebratory dinner. After a full day of other business meetings with some of the clients of Daktronics displays on Times Square and at other New York locations, and an evening at the New York Islanders-Tampa Lighting hockey game, Kurtenbach and his wife of forty four years left the hustle and bustle of New York and boarded a Northwestern flight at Laguardia. They were happy with their visit but eager to get back to their beloved South Dakota.

As the jetliner climbed to altitude and the Kurtenbachs settled in for the uneventful flight back to mid-America, the then nearly 70-year-old visionary subconsciously massaged his long-suffering knee that Prince, the coal black gelding pony who was almost like a member of the Kurtenbach family, had fallen on so many years ago. He thought proudly about the morning's events that added even more prestige and visibility to the remarkable company that he and Sander had created in their minds and then nurtured and coaxed along over smooth and bumpy roads in the early years.

Kurtenbach and Sander and their wives had discussed and debated the possibilities of starting a company of some type for months as they sat in either the Sander or Kurtenbach kitchen sipping coffee and consuming too many home-baked cookies. The plan contained a penciled-in notation of a "stock offering" the four somewhat innocently assumed would occur a decade after the company was formed. It didn't quite work out that way. The public offering of Daktronics stock had taken place in 1994. And now, more than thirty-five years had passed since those late-night and weekend coffee klatches in Brookings, and since the first Daktonics product, an ingenious-for-its-time solid-state electronic voting system for the Utah Legislature, made its public debut. It had been carted out of the twenty by twenty foot Daktronics manufacturing office that was no bigger than the milk separator room back on the Kurtenbach farm. Now the firm had, on all levels, far exceeded the prophesies set down in the coffee-stained rough draft of the business plan developed so many years ago. Incidentally, because Daktronics at that time had limited funds, Kurtenbach reached an agreement with building owner Orville Duff to pay rent in the form of Daktronics shares, which as their value grew and split several times, turned out for Duff to be a very profitable deal. With the voting machine installed in Utah, what was believed by many doubters and detractors to be a company with a daunting prospect of success had now far exceeded what was first envisioned in the Kurtenbach and Sander kitchens.

This trip to New York was a joyous occasion indeed. Not a bad day for a somewhat reticent former farm kid from South Dakota who still relished his privacy and the solitude of country life and who, until after he graduated from high school in Parkston near his hometown of Dimock, had never been more than 150 miles from home. Since Daktronics was formed, of course, Kurtenbach logged hundreds of thousands of miles by land, sea, and air. He'd traveled to the four corners, established satellite offices, given speeches and university lectures, served in the South Dakota Legislature and on the state's Board of Regents, accepted a plethora of awards and honors for his innovative work, and just traveled for pleasure as he often dreamed he would. Those dreams of worldwide travel had helped make the long hours in the 1940s and 1950s on the farm go faster as he bounced along on the putt-putting B John Deere tractor or guided kind and gentle Barney and Chub, the family's ponderous work horses with hooves big as pie tins, on their never-ending, circuitous pull around fertile corn and wheat fields.

He was a sophomore in high school before his first long journey of any note. That was when he and a few others from the Parkston High School FFA Chapter traveled to the state Future Farmers of America convention at South Dakota State University in Brookings where he would eventually teach. His first trip outside the State of South Dakota was after he enlisted for a four-year tour in the United States Air Force in 1954. The Korean War had cooled down, but some of the details of a difficult peace treaty were being worked out with the North Koreans at Panmunjom, so there was a call to duty. And now, with a more global outlook that the Air Force service helped to instill in him, his company had gained international recognition, acceptance, and accolades. He was at the pinnacle of success. As the jet continued west into the sunset bound for Sioux Falls, he thought of his mother and father, and of his roots that coursed deep into the flat, fertile, and often fickle farmland in northern Hutchinson County, South Dakota.

Kurtenbach was born and grew up on the farm homesteaded by his grandparents, Ferdinand and Christina Kurtenbach. It was only a five-minute bareback pony ride from the farmstead of his paternal great grandparents, Johann Wilhelm and Elizabeth Kurtenbach from Vettelschoss, Germany, about seventy-five miles from Frankfort. Ferdinand and Christina were also born in Germany and came to America in the 1880s to start a new life. Aelred never met them. Christina died a decade before his birth, and Ferdinand died in late 1932, two years before he was born.

Ferdinand was born in March of 1855 in Orscheid, Cologne, Germany, one of nine children of Johann Wilhelm and Elizabeth Kurtenbach. Ferdinand's future wife, Christina Gratzfeld, was born in June 1858 in Wulscheid, Germany. Both immigrated to America when in their twenties. Ferdinand's parents, all of Ferdinand's six brothers, and one of his two sisters eventually came to America. Ferdinand and his brothers John and Peter came first, in 1883, to settle in Hutchinson County, South Dakota. They arrived at a propitious period in what history books now describe as The Great Dakota Boom. Economic times were good and thousands of new settlers were arriving in the territory, tripling the population in just two years. The boys' mother, father, and the others arrived in the new state of South Dakota in 1889 and were granted citizenship in 1895. John, the brother who had arrived earlier with Ferdinand, Pete and sister Elizabeth, later left Hutchinson County to begin a new life in Canada. But the other Kurtenbachs remained in the Dimock area all of their lives.

What brought the Johann Kurtenbach family to America? A combination of things, including poverty, what the Kurtenbachs perceived as a decline in morality that unemployment often creates, and the military and social shenanigans of the country's leadership.

As young men in Germany, Ferdinand, Aelred's grandfather, and Ferdinand's brothers often thought about their future and the prospects of making their way in their homeland. The future looked bleak. The only work available consisted of menial tasks such waiting on others or such things as picking rocks from the fields and pastures of wealthy landowners. The country seemed constantly at war with neighbors through most of the 1860s and at war with France beginning in 1870. War and the drafting of young men to fight seemed never far away. Ferdinand and his two brothers were at or approaching compulsory military age, so surely some or all of them would find themselves in the German army sooner or later.

The prospect of the killing fields, or waiting to be called to war, especially in a time of high unemployment and low wages, caused social ills, as well. With sad hearts the Kurtenbach family watched as other young men around them turned to liquor as a temporary escape and a relief from the monotony and the dreary life in Germany at that time. It was a tempting avenue for even the Kurtenbach boys to pursue, but they chose otherwise.

Also weighing heavily on the minds of many Germans, including Ferdinand and the others, was the rule of Otto van Bismarck. Among Chancellor Bismarck's political objectives was a program aimed at reducing the influence of the Catholic Church in Germany. So as devout Catholics, the Kurtenbachs likely also sought refuge in America in part because of this attempt at sociological engineering in their home country.

The Kurtenbach family had listened as others in the shops, markets, and the church waxed enthusiastic about the free land in America that could be acquired through what was called The Homestead Act of 1862. John, Ferdinand, and Peter, the three oldest boys, decided to seek this plentiful bounty in Dakota Territory, where many of their compatriots had ventured in earlier years. Once established in the new world, they would write back to their parents, Johann Wilhelm and Elizabeth, about the prospects for the rest of the family joining them. They were the advance contingent for the rest of their family, who would attempt passage later when more about The Homestead Act was known and when the younger Kurtenbach children were able to better withstand the rigorous voyage across the Atlantic Ocean.

So with little money but unbounded hope, the Kurtenbach brothers left their family and made the trip to America, arriving in early 1883 with other Germans. South Dakota would not gain statehood for another six years.

After a difficult ocean voyage, the young men rode rattling, swaying trains to Scotland, South Dakota, and then walked the approximately 45 miles to the Dimock area. At first, they earned their keep and a few extra dollars working for others. After locating suitable land, Aelred's grandfather Ferdinand applied for a homestead (No. 7664), filing in Olivet, Dakota Territory, on July 7, 1883. His homestead choice was for 166.88 acres of land he had staked out (legally identified as Lots Two, Three, and Four and the south one-half of the northwest one-fourth of Section nine in Township 100 of range 60 west). He returned to that land after filing his application for homestead and set about proving up, one of the requirements for eventual ownership. Earlier, with a borrowed breaking plow, he cut into virgin soil and lifted out lengths of sod to make a crude, tiny hut for protection from the elements. It had no windows, and its ill-fitting door, initially supported by leather hinges, kept out most of the scudding snow that in the winter forever fell and drifted with the wind, searching for the low and sheltered places, building into huge, packed drifts.

In that first year on his own as a farmer, Ferdinand planted thirty acres of wheat, oats, and flax. In 1885, he had fifty acres planted to wheat, oats, flax, corn, and potatoes, and by the following year he was working eighty acres, reaching his recorded 110 acres of crop land in 1889. Records show that during that period, he paid between $6 and $9 a year in property taxes on these acres. In 1888, with this early preparatory work completed, and with some money saved, he sent for his sweetheart and future wife, Christina Gratzfeld. With the money he provided, and some more cash the Gratzfelds had saved, Christina, 30 years old, came to America and she married Ferdinand in Dimock in May1888.

By the time of the infamous killer blizzard of 1888, in which 112 people in the southern half of Dakota Territory perished, Ferdinand and Christina were living safe and sound in a tiny wood frame house he had built. After the blizzard, temperatures dropped to minus thirty degrees and livestock and wildlife losses in the state mounted. Industrious, and blessed with that famous German penchant for thrift, the young couple were scathed but determined, and the next spring broke sod and planted a few more acres of wheat and potatoes to tide them over.

They would survive, be a part of the territory's transition into the State of South Dakota, and become respected leaders in their community and in the church that meant to much to the early education and training of the future founder of Daktronics.

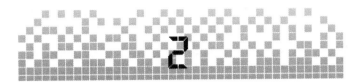

New Generations

Two weeks before Christmas 1888, as part of the homesteading requirement, Aelred's grandfather Ferdinand Kurtenbach buggied to Mitchell in Davison County to apply for citizenship. He traveled with two friends from the Dimock area he'd selected as witnesses, William Koch and Engelbert Schlimgen. His friends sat nearby as he stood nervously before District Judge Bartlett Tripp. When Ferdinand signed his citizen papers, he renounced, as did every immigrant, "all allegiance and fidelity to every foreign prince, potentate, state or sovereignty whatever, and more particularly the Emperor of Germany." Reference to the German emperor was a caveat added to address specifics as to country of origin for all applicants from all countries. Ferdinand treasured those citizenship papers. He kept them within easy reach all of his life, to proudly inspect and admire. In his later years he asked that they remain in the custody of his son John, Aelred's father.

The next year, 1889, with Dakota Territory divided into two states, Ferdinand broke more ground and planted more crops, repeating the cycle each year. He would eventually become a very successful farmer and a wealthy man.

The following year, 1890, Ferdinand returned to the Davison County Courthouse to fill out the customary Homestead, Pre-Emption and Commutation Proof, a questionnaire intended to prove that the applicant had met, proved up as they called it, the requirements for homestead. Among other things, Ferdinand—in his own handwriting—indicated "in October 1883 built a sod house and dug a well…" In another section he wrote that he built his first house in October 1883 and "in June 1884 I built the house I now reside in." He described the house as being twelve by eighteen feet plus an addition of eight by fourteen feet. The wood frame house, he said, "had a pine floor, cellar below, lathed, plastered and painted." He estimated its value at $250. He also listed a twelve by thirty-two foot barn valued at $60; a sixteen by twenty foot granary valued at $75; a sixteen by twenty foot machine shed having a value of $40; a chicken house estimated to be worth $50; two wells, "both curbed," worth $65; fifteen acres fenced, five and one-half acres of trees, together valued at $260; and one hundred-ten acres of farm land valued at $320.

Among equipment he had acquired was a self-binder, mower, hayrack, plow, harrow, fanning mill, of which he owned one-half share with another farmer, and "small tools," to which he added "....had some in the beginning and added some every year."

The questionnaire also asked what household goods he and his wife owned. His listing included "two beds and bedding, cradle, stove, two tables, three chairs, two kitchen cupboards, clock, looking glass and cooking materials." To this list he added: "Had some when I was a batchelor (sic.) and bought some when I got married." This document was duly registered and a copy sent to the United States Land Office in Yankton at which time his original filing, Number 7664, was approved. Ferdinand proudly paid a $4 fee and in May 1890 became owner of the original 166.88 acres. He was at that time thirty-five years old, only slightly older than his future grandson, Aelred, would be when he launched Daktronics.

Even in those very early days, the Catholic Church that marked the western limits of what became the town of Dimock was a refuge and a sanctuary for the German immigrant pioneers of the area. That was especially so during and in the aftermath of the Blizzard of 1888 that had swooped down on the land beginning on January 12th. The spring thaw after that killer storm left Ferdinand's low land inundated, along with thousand of other acres in the Dimock area. And if the ravages of the weather and the aftermath of winters weren't enough, there was the abomination of the grasshopper hordes, disease, and accidental injury that were common. Croup, dropsy, acute diarrhea, cancer, diphtheria, cholera, lung fever, and bronchitis, not to mention sunstroke and heart attacks were the most common afflictions. Horses kicked and cattle gored. Even a simple infection from a tiny scratch or puncture wound could be fatal. The church helped the people survive all of this, and more.

But even with the church standing with them, when faced with such a hard, difficult life, it was easy to become discouraged. Many gave up, saying they had "seen the elephant," which was a common adage of the day, a descriptive way to speak of the immensity of the landscape and the enormity of the challenge. Ferdinand and Christina were not turning back. While they, too, may have had a glimpse of the elephant, they were determined to work through the difficulties and the vicissitudes of pioneering, and to make a new life for themselves and their growing family.

The psychological stresses must have been as punishing as the physical demands and privations. At the time, nearly eighty percent of the approximately 10,000 people living in Hutchinson County were German-Americans. So Hutchinson County, for those German-Americans, was a welcome safe harbor from the isolation and loneliness that defeated so many other pioneers. It offered security in an often-difficult and demanding land. Help and support from fellow Germans was always a short walk or wagon ride away.

And the church, too, provided a welcome reprieve from the hard work and the disappointments. It was a spiritual haven and a social meeting place, bringing members of the parish together to celebrate the neighborhood's successes and mourn its losses. Living in Dakota Territory was then, for Ferdinand and Christina Kurtenbach and for Aelred's maternal grandparents Nicholas and Eva Mayer, and for every pioneer around them, a hardscrabble existence. Somehow, they managed, and they found strength, solace, and support holding hands, rubbing shoulders, and praying with the other German families in the neighborhood and in their church. Together they adopted a new culture that was a combination of German and American customs and traditions. And they slowly learned the English language, although certain German phrases remained part of the language of these new immigrants.

Ferdinand and Christina Kurtenbach had ten children, all born in the wood frame home that had eventually replaced the hut of sod. Included in their family were three sets of twins, among them Aelred Kurtenbach's father John, and John's twin sister, Christina, both of whom arrived in the new world June 2, 1890. Two years after their birth, Frank and Joseph were born Sept. 15, 1892, died as infants; and five years later, on the last day of June 1897, twins Ella and Otto joined the family. An indication of the diffi-

13

cult life on the prairie is the fact that only four of their children lived past childhood. Meanwhile, a few miles southwest of the Kurtenbach home, Aelred's maternal grandparents, Nicholas and Eva Mayer, raised a family of fifteen children.

This was a time of drought in the state, and the dry conditions continued into the middle of the 1890s. In the year Aelred's father was born, the population of South Dakota was 328,808. Living in the state at the time were 18,188 German-born citizens. A good share of them lived in and around Hutchinson County.

Ferdinand and Christina settled in the Dimock area (known as Rome) too late to help in the building of the community's first Catholic Church in 1882. It was set down on a foundation of fieldstone picked off the virgin prairie land near a blacksmith shop and a creamery that served farmers in the immediate area. The land was donated by Engelbert Schlimgen and Lawrence and Sybilla Bowar. Engelbert Schlimgen, incidentally, would later appear as a friend and witness at the granting of citizenship to Ferdinand.

As might be expected, that first church was small with spartan amenities. At the time, the Milwaukee Railroad passed through town but didn't stop in the little village because of the railroad's desire to locate depots about twelve miles apart on the assumption that farmers bringing produce by horse-drawn wagon for rail shipment could make a haul of six miles in and six miles back to the farm in a day. Rome was situated halfway between

Tiny Dimock's main drag in 1912.

Ethan and Parkston. Later, as the town grew, adding new businesses and towering, sturdy elevators for holding tons of grain for shipment when larger quantities had accumulated, the railroad built a small depot and the whistle stop became Starr because it was located in Starr Township.

There was apparently another place named Starr somewhere on the rail line, so in 1911 officials of the Chicago, Milwaukee and St. Paul line renamed the village Dimock. History isn't entirely clear as to the town's namesake. Some historic writings indicate it was named after a Mr. Dimock, who surveyed the original rail bed through town. But the prevailing theory is that the Dimock name honored a dedicated and popular Hutchinson County public servant, Warren Dimock, who was county State's Attorney from 1891 to 1906 and later represented his mostly German-American constituency in the South Dakota Legislature before becoming a county judge. As Dimock grew to its hey-day in the late 1920s and early 1930s, it would eventually boast of having a hotel, hardware store, blacksmith shop, bowling alley, hat shop, theater, café, gas station, garage, saloon, car sales lot and a huge implement dealership, three grain elevators, jail, and cheese factory, which fostered a tradition of cheese making in the community that continues today.

Before most of those businesses were established, that first Catholic Church in Dimock was moved from its field stone footings a few rods to the east, which is the site of today's imposing Sts. Peter and Paul Catholic Church.

The late 1800s and on into the 1900s were times of prairie fires, feared even more by the pioneers than the numbing blizzards of winter and the whirling tornados of spring and fall. It was not uncommon for the smoke of prairie fires to roll up in giant clouds on the far horizon and glow red through the night, fed by an infernal appetite for dry buffalo and Indian grass. Lightning was often the culprit, but man, too, could lose control of home fires, and coal-dust-covered engine tenders on locomotives passing through might accidentally send sparks out onto tinder-dry grass along the track. Without the barriers of road or water or bare plowed ground, flames fanned by the unending Dakota winds danced out of control, often consuming dozens of square miles of farmland and the structures upon it before burning themselves out.

It was a stabbing lightning bolt, not a prairie fire, that sparked the end of the first little Catholic Church in what was then Rome. The bolt found sustenance on the dry wood frame of that church and left smoldering timbers and damage that was considered beyond repair. The loss did not deter parish members. They had often faced heart-breaking disappointment and temporary defeat in their daily lives, so they did not despair. If anything, they came together for a common purpose. Aelred's grandparents, Ferdinand and Christina, Nicholas and Eva, and the others of the parish built a new wood-framed edifice twice the size of the original building. Then, in 1908, that church also burned to the ground, this time from unknown causes. All that was saved was the church bell, heavily sooted, but still sound.

Parishioners rallied once more, Aelred's grandparents among them. Members voted to build a structure that would not be as susceptible to fire. They would erect one that would be strong against the elements and able to survive for their children, their grandchildren, and parishioners far into the future. And they would put up an edifice that would be an inspiration to all who would see it. At that time, the Chicago, Milwaukee and St. Paul Railroad had been completed from Scotland to the south and Mitchell to the north, and in 1907, church officials persuaded the rail line to build a spur line of a half-mile so the massive amount of materials and construction sup-

Grain elevators in Dimock along the north-south railroad track.

plies could be transported directly to the church building site.

Beneficence reigned and everyone felt duty-bound to help. Ferdinand and Christina Kurtenbach and their neighbors, Nick and Eva Mayer, the Peter Arnsbergs, the Herbert Zehnpfennings and all of the rest, contributed their time, their labor, and their hard-earned money to pay for the construction of this larger and more beautiful, pink-red brick building on the same ground that had been donated years before by Englebert Schlimgen. It would cost $34,000, all of it pledged and all of those pledges paid in full by parish members even before the church was completed.

With the rail spur in and building materials stacked nearby, proud members of the parish gathered on a cold, sunless October day in 1908 to set in the corner stone. A photograph of the occasion shows white haired old men and strong, handsome young men and boys, all with heads bared, and women and children smartly dressed to the nines in their Sunday best, bundled warmly against a brisk wind. They stand, aligned on the low scaffolding and in the litter of chipped brick and mortar at the work site. Behind them is a large cloth banner depicting Joseph and Baby Jesus. They worshipped there in the cold wind at the site of the beginnings of the church's south-facing entry, all sharing in the joy of the day with the four acolytes and three priests and a bishop who conducted the outdoor service.

The Sts. Peter and Paul Catholic Church and school, where Aelred and his brothers and sisters attended their first eighth grades. The cemetery is to the left of the church.

17

In the crowd were Ferdinand and Christina Kurtenbach and Nicholas and Eva Mayer, Aelred's grandparents. So, too, were their children, John Kurtenbach and Theodora Mayer, who would one day marry and become Aelred's parents.

The new Sts. Peter and Paul Catholic Church and most of the intricate and delicate artwork within its walls were completed by July 1909. Viewed from the air, the church is built in the shape of a huge cross. It is indeed the imposing, inspirational building the parishioners had envisioned. Aelred Kurtenbach's life, and the lives of all of his relatives and their friends were entwined with that church from 1909 to the present day.

As did many other parishioners, Aelred Kurtenbach's grandparents Ferdinand and Christina pledged $550 to the church building fund. His maternal grandparents Nicholas and Eva Mayer contributed $500. Ferdinand and Christina later gave $25 for a stained glass church window, and then donated $46.50 for the XIII Station of the Cross. The very first donors to the Stations of the Cross fund drive were Aelred's maternal grandparents Nicholas and Eva Mayer, who also gave $46.50. Later, they contributed $25 for the church's St. Nicholas statue. Everyone—including a handful of non-Catholics in the Dimock area—gave what they could afford. Gifts and pledges ranged from $10 to $700 (to the donor, the $10 pledge may have been more of the family budget than the high pledge of $700 designated by a more wealthy parishioner). An idea of the extent of those donations can be better understood by considering that the average assessed value of an acre of land in Hutchinson County was less than $5 at that time.

In a brief history of the church commemorating its Centennial in 1985, Aelred's maternal grandparents are singled out for having provided "the most outstanding example of sacrifice for the parish." Nicholas and Eva Mayer made room in their small farm home southwest of Dimock for five or six of the Benedictine nuns awaiting completion of a home for the nuns near the church. The Mayers not only provided free room and board, but they brought the nuns by team and wagon to and from the church and school each day for six months.

Five years after the stoneworkers and church artisans had left and the spur rail line had been torn up, parishioners under the direction of Father John Wulf began construction of a new, three-story brick Sts. Peter and

Paul Catholic School. It would replace an old wood frame structure no longer big enough to hold a growing enrollment.

While it was probably a matter of available space rather than planning, the locations of the new school and the church cemetery seemed symbolic. The brick school were Aelred and his brothers and sisters attended their first eight grades was built on the east, the sunrise side of the new church. To the imme-diate west of the church, on the sunset side, is the cemetery that

Aelred Kurtenbach at the graves of his paternal grandparents, Ferdinand and Christina, Sts. Peter and Paul Catholic Cemetery, Dimock.

each day catches the final warming rays of the setting Dakota sun. It is in this cemetery where a host of Kurtenbachs are buried, those who were first to ar-rive and progeny of that early contingent who have since been called home, including Aelred Kurtenbach's paternal and maternal great grandparents, his grandparents, and his parents, John and Theodora.

Those parish symbols—the school and the cemetery—and Sts. Peter and Paul Church itself, have since 1909 never been far from the eyes and minds of parishioners of yesterday and today. The church is at the parish's fulcrum, visible from farm house and field for miles around. The surviving old church bell that once was activated by muscle power and a long rope from the bell tower to the interior church balcony is now electronically operated. Its clar-ion call can still be heard for miles, and it still tolls as it did for early settlers, many too poor to own a watch or a mantle clock, the beginning of each day at 6 a.m. The bell sounds again at high noon and then at 6 p.m.

In earlier days, it also announced deaths, pealing once for each year of the life of the deceased as soon as the news of the passing reached the parish priest, so that those friends and neighbors who avidly kept abreast of the health and well being of one another, could know or have a good idea for whom the bell was tolling. Today, that tradition has been modified. The bell

Sts. Peter and Paul Church and Cemetery, Dimock.

now tolls the age of the deceased as the cortege escorts the casket the short distance to the nearby cemetery on the sunset side of the church.

The church's steeple and its cross finial are prominent, looming over the corn and bean fields that reach out in all directions. From the site where Aelred's great grandparents Wilhelm and Elizabeth first settled, which now consists of a few stubborn, gnarled Chinese elm trees, a sparse but determined cedar tree, a few faint paths and driveways, and two old buildings that have fallen in on themselves, the steeple is clearly visible to the southwest. It is there, just as it was for Aelred's grandparents, Ferdinand and Christina adjacent to Wilhelm and Elizabeth's farmstead one hundred years ago, where their son John and his wife Theodora raised their family. It beckons from wherever one might stand on the same farmyard where Aelred Kurtenbach was born and grew up. The steeple fairly dominates the flatness of the land, a pinnacle amidst the horizontal landscape. It was and remains today at the center of that farming community's universe. It was there when the co-founder of Daktronics was growing up just as it had been there for the progeny of those other early German-American pioneers on surrounding farms.

All have felt the steeple's gravitational pull; all have been drawn to the church and its teachings by that high, white cross filial tall as a man, and by the cross-shaped church below it. Ferdinand and Christina now rest below that cross with other Kurtenbachs in the nearby cemetery. Surely the heritage they brought and the precepts and rubrics of hard work and honesty they lived by are now reflected in the Daktronics philosophy as fostered by Aelred Kurtenbach.

When Ferdinand and Christina's son, the twin John Kurtenbach, grew up and became a farmer, he did not travel far from home. The father of Aelred Kurtenbach acquired his father's land that by then had been expanded from the original 166.88 acres to 206 acres of field and pasture. It was there that John and his first wife, Elizabeth Mayer, who was born near Dimock on Dec. 6, 1886, settled to raise a family: three daughters, Marie, born in 1916; Magdalen, born in 1919; Marcellina, born in 1921; and a son Wilfred, born in 1918.

Sadly, John's wife Elizabeth died a few days before Christmas in 1930. Cancer was suspected. In early 1932, a still-mourning John Kurtenbach married Elizabeth's sister Theodora Mayer, then 31-years-old. They had nine children, three girls and six boys. Seven more of Theodora and John's nine children followed Aelred and older brother John (Jack), the couple's first born, who had arrived on Sept. 14, 1932. Three more of the "Dirty

The Kurtenbach farm home near Dimock, SD.

Thirties" kids were boys, Denis, born June 4, 1935; DeWayne, born October 9, 1936; and Frank, born September 10, 1937. Eva broke the male dominance, arriving April 23, 1939. Their seventh child was Ivan, born September 15, 1940, followed by Alice, on February 13, 1943. Rita, the last, was born December 11, 1945.

This extended family of Kurtenbachs, thirteen in all including the four children from John's earlier marriage, quite literally filled the Kurtenbach farmhouse stem to stern. Other than that, it was a typical South Dakota farmhouse: nothing fancy, sited on a slight, natural rise of land and built sturdy in the wood frame fashion on a fieldstone foundation, two stories high, with a wide porch facing the barn. Crowded into it was a loving family, and their numbers helped foster a respect for one another and taught them the need for teamwork that became a Kurtenbach family trademark. And it probably gave Aelred Kurtenbach the inspiration and pointed the way for the unique and remarkably successful company that he would eventually, against all the odds, establish.

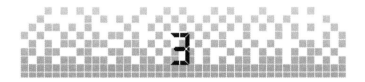

Farming's Early Lessons

King, the dutiful workhorse and the Kurtenbach Model T Ford each had a part in the birth of Aelred Kurtenbach.

The future co-founder of Daktronics, Inc., was born in the cold, crisp early morning of Wednesday, January 3, 1934. As the impending birth drew near, Aelred's parents, John and Theodora, decided the time had come for John to get one of Theodora's older sisters to help move the process along.

So late on the night of Tuesday, January 2, John buttoned up his sheepskin greatcoat and walked on crunching snow to the car shed he'd nailed to the Kurtenbach granary. John fetched the car's crank from the trunk. As he guessed, the stubborn old flivver refused to start no matter how forcefully he turned the crank or how sternly he lectured it with a few "Mein Gotts" and other terse phrases in German or English that he seldom uttered except to catch the undivided attention of stubbon pigs or wayward cows.

Casting the rusted crank aside, opted to Plan B and walked the few steps to the barn. It was dark, but he harnessed King from memory of a thousand other hitches on a thousand other dark mornings. King was hitched to the rear bumper of the car, and John slid into the driver's seat. He took in a deep gulp of cold air, adjusted the magneto and choke levers just right, put the gear shift to reverse and clapped his gloved hands together for good luck. Gripping the steering wheel, he yelled "giddyap King!" The faithful horse lurched forward. The car tires popped loose of the grasping ice and slowly turned. Then at just the right moment at just the right speed, John popped the clutch. The old car wheezed, coughed a few times, and started. John "whoaed" King, who was more than happy to comply, and both waited a moment or two just in case the old Ford wasn't serious about continuing to run. It was, and John had one less worry on this important night.

He unhitched King, and with a slap on the rump that stirred up a small cloud of stable dust, the old workhouse trotted back, still in harness, to the comfort of his familiar stall. After the short drive to Aunt Lollie Bowar's place, and now with the car parked on a slight incline outside the Kurtenbach house in the event it would be needed again, all that was left was the waiting. The country doctor had been called earlier from Mitchell a few miles away and now he, too, was there.

Aelred was delivered, not full of woe as Wednesday's children are predicted to be, but kicking and crying and weighing in at a healthy twelve pounds. The sun was just clearing the eastern horizon on January 3, 1934. It wasn't the most propitious time for a future entrepreneur to enter the world. The summer after his birth, the dreadful depression and asphyxiating dust storms still swirled over the midwest. Like wolves stalking an injured animal, grasshopper hordes waited for the dust to settle and then flew in to eat most everything that hadn't blown away or been buried under the swirling dirt.

Later that month of his birth, the new Kurtenbach boy, the second child of John and Theodora, was baptized Aelred Joseph in the beautiful Sts. Peter and Paul Catholic Church, the pride of Dimock. His mother Theodora later told him she selected the name Aelred because a Saint Aelred was the patron saint of integrity, and also because in her younger years in Parkston she babysat a little boy by that name, the son of one of the owners of the Corner Café where she worked as a waitress. Theodora was a very religious person, and she liked the little boy she watched over, so Aelred was the special name she picked for her Wednesday's child. She didn't believe in nicknames for any of her children, and never once did she shorten Aelred to just plain "Al."

In 1935, about a year after Aelred's birth, President Franklin D. Roosevelt was searching for federal programs that might help mitigate the terrible economic conditions, especially in rural America where the bite was particularly painful. He created the Rural Electric Administration in 1935. That good idea slowly began to change the rural scene, lighting the farms and lightening the farmers' heavy load. By the time Aelred entered high school in Parkston, rural electrification had changed the quality of life for everyone on the farm. Electricity made it all happen, of course, and it was also the mysterious physical phenomena that drew Aelred, as a student and later as an entrepreneur, into the successful career he was destined to experience.

As Aelred grew, he and his older brother Jack, and eventually the other Kurtenbach children, came to know every inch of that 206-acre piece of Dakota flatland as well as the backs of their hands, from building to pasture badger holes. Dimock and the surrounding farmlands were the center of the universe for them and the children settled into the comforting rhythm of the farming seasons and learned the lessons of life on the farm. For Aelred, those lessons would prove useful and valuable for later life, and he applied many of his early experiences and lessons into the business plan as he and his wife Irene worked with Duane and Phyllis Sander to co-found the successful Daktronics, Inc., in 1968.

Aelred and younger brother Denis enjoying free rides around the farm home, compliments of Jack.

He learned what teamwork can accomplish and what caring people naturally do for one another, such as his memory of a nearly disastrous fire on the farm that remains clear in his mind today. It happened on an otherwise uneventful, quiet Sunday afternoon in October 1939 when he was five years old. The family's hired man Walter Puetz ran into the house hollering that the barn was on fire. John and his oldest son Wilfred hurried out to the barn to investigate and do what they could until more help arrived. Theodora Kurtenbach called neighbors on the party line telephone shared by eleven other nearby farm families.

Internal combustion in some recently chopped corn fodder had started the smoldering fire. It spread to dried corn stalks nearby, and that sent the flames up toward the haymow. There was a very real possibility of losing the barn and its contents. Neighbors began arriving in what seemed like minutes after the phone call for help went out. It was determined that the smoldering fodder that had been spread out several inches thick in an area of the barn needed to be removed. It was carried out with scoop shovels or whatever was handy, and spread on the ground, then doused with buckets of water dipped from the stock tank. Doing that, and smothering what was afire in other areas of the barn, took until about 11 p.m. Hours before, neighbor ladies had arrived with sandwiches and refreshments for the Kurtenbach children and the fire fighters. A disaster had been averted. "It still amazes me how that all took place," Aelred said. "The response by our neighbors was so rapid and everyone was so willing to drop everything and come to our assistance."

There were other lessons of teamwork and neighborliness, too. When Aelred was a freshman in high school in nearby Parkston, he was disappointed on Thursday that it was a school day and he couldn't accompany his father to the farm of neighbor and son-in-law Verlin (Pat) Walz. Twenty-six other farmers gathered there to harvest Walz's fifty-five acres of corn while Walz recovered from an injury. The day before, John drove his tractor to the George Funke farm after learning of George's hospitalization. He and thirty-three other neighbors made short work of the thirty-five-acre corn field. Then they toasted their success and their friend's full recovery with bottles of cold beer that Al's Bar in Dimock contributed to the harvest bee.

Aelred is a man with a good balance of rural life and small town living. He has unpretentious tastes. He is reserved and incurably optimistic, believing in the future. He remembers the lessons he learned from helpful friends and neighbors at barn and field fires, plowing bees and at other times of need. These precepts are the basis for many of the philosophies embedded within his company's culture.

As Aelred grew he contracted—as might be expected in a large family—the usual procession of childhood diseases that marched from home to home in the 1930s. He also suffered from one particularly long and painful condition caused by infected mastoids. Padding had to be pinned to the shoulders of his shirts to soak up the nearly constant drainage from his ears. He recovered from that with no apparent damage to his hearing, although later in life his wife Irene occasionally takes joking issue with that.

Scarlet fever visited the Kurtenbach household when Aelred was in the second grade. He and his younger brother Denis came down with the disease, and as a precaution the doctor quarantined the entire family. He told Mrs. Kurtenbach to give her sick children plenty of liquids so she stocked up on bottles of Seven-Up. It was the first time Aelred or his brothers and sisters had ever tasted a soft drink, and it was considered a special treat, not something having medicinal qualities. Whenever the supply of Seven-Up dwindled because the other children had to try it, too, the substitute that his mother decided to serve was a glass of what the boys laughingly dubbed Seven-Down. It was sauerkraut juice dipped from the barrel of that German delicacy stored in big, heavy crocks, covered with a board held in place by a heavy field stone, in the coolness of the basement. When all else failed, the two youngsters got to share a bottle of beer. But just one.

An injury that is still picture-clear in Aelred's mind's eye happened when he was ten years old. He was put in charge of the family poultry crew whose responsibilities included feeding and watering the family flock

Aelred aboard Prince, the Kurtenbach family pet and pony.

Busy at farm chores, Aelred, left, and older brother Jack.

of partly grown baby chicks. His apprentices were eight-year-old DeWayne and seven-year-old Frank. Aelred sent them to the barn for a bucket of oats to fill the feeder. When they didn't return soon enough, he climbed on the chicken pen fence so he could see over a slight rise in the farmyard to determine the cause of their delay. His foot slipped on the fence and he fell on his side. His mother determined his left arm was broken.

Aelred's father drove him to Dr. William Reib's office in Parkston, and Dr. Reib took them in his fancy car to the hospital where he administered a mild anesthetic to dull the re-setting pain. The drug didn't agree with Aelred's constitution. Riding back to the Kurtenbach car after the procedure, Aelred felt groggy and queasy. His stomach erupted mightily, and needless to say, the doctor's nice automobile required a good cleaning, much to embarrassment of both Aelred and his father.

During the summer of 1944 between Aelred's fourth and fifth grades, the Kurtenbach boys were successful in convincing their father that a pony would be a good investment. It could help the boys when fetching or herding cattle. On a horse, they argued, they could get quickly from one farm chore to the next. It is doubtful their father bought their arguments, but he did get them a pony named Prince. The friendly little horse remained a part of the Kurtenbach family for the next twenty years.

Riding Prince didn't always go as planned. In the summer of 1946, Aelred, then twelve, and Prince were in the one hundred acre north cow pasture checking cattle. They came upon a heifer having difficulty delivering her first calf. Aelred dug his heels into Prince's sides and they raced for home and help. At full speed over an area known to be claimed by burrowing badgers, Prince stepped into a tunnel entrance and fell. Aelred's right leg was caught under Prince's side as the two skidded along on the ground. It was painful, but Prince was up in a flash and Aelred limped over to the pony and remounted. The two continued pell-mell to the house. Help was alerted, but it arrived too late to save the heifer and her calf. The injury to Aelred's knee was serious, but no bones were broken. However, to this day, that bum knee often reminds him of Prince and the hard spill in the north cow pasture.

Especially with boys, arguments were inevitable, although Aelred remembered that the brothers got along surprisingly well most of the time. A memorable exception happened one stormy day when the children were playing in the girls' room, the big upstairs bedroom. Denis took issue with Aelred over something now long forgotten. He grabbed a croquet mallet as an equalizer. Aelred took flight for the stairs and the safe haven in the living room where their father was reading the weekly *Parkston Advance*. But he wasn't quite fast enough. The mallet caught him square on the back of the head. Blood spurted and Aelred howled. His parents calmly shaved blond hair from around the gash and then carefully applied the thin membrane from the inside of a fresh egg to the wound. It was Theodora's cure-all. The egg shell swatch was taped in place and when it dried, it shrunk, pulling the wound together. The calamity ended with apologies from Denis.

The Kurtenbach brothers Denis, Jack, DeWayne and Aelred.

When Aelred was younger, before his important assignment as superintendent of chicken feeding, he and his brothers and sisters were confined close by the house by a wire fence. It kept the curious kids away from horse hooves, cow horns, hog snouts, and a plethora of pitfalls that a curious child could surely find on a busy farm.

During the 1930s, additions to the family arrived like clockwork almost every year. At times as many as a half-dozen Kurtenbach kids could be playing in the fenced yard. Games

Billy, the lone saddle horse on the Kurtenbach farm, with Jack at the reins, and Aelred, holding on tight.

were invented and turns taken for space in the sandbox or for riding the replica toy ice truck that was Aelred's first gift from a kindly aunt. With all of the kids taking turns, that peddle truck traveled with reckless abandon along the narrow sidewalk that followed the contours of the big home's fieldstone foundation, careening at times into their mother's geraniums, peonies, and hollyhocks, for which they were sternly reprimanded.

Toys of any kind were at a premium in those difficult economic times. The playthings that did arrive at the Kurtenbach home were put to extreme proving ground tests by the often raucous children. Most of the toys did not survive unscathed for long. Aelred recalls that they always seemed to lose a wheel, drop a bolt, or snap in two.

As the children grew older, the yard gate was opened and their playground was expanded to include all

Future tractor operators Aelred, left, and brother Jack.

206 acres. So, too, did their work assignments grow in responsiblity.

As the chores became more difficult, the play became more daring, too. A tall combination corn crib/granary was a favorite haunt and a huge challenge to the Kurtenbach boys. They explored the ingenious grain chutes and activating levers devised by skilled German-American carpenters and craftsmen. They sought its heights, racing up wooden ladders to the cupola while the others counted the seconds needed for the trip. They careened from joist to joist twenty or more feet in the air and cavorted recklessly on two-by-four boards like tight-rope walkers. Their mother's hair gradually turned white with worry.

When not climbing corn crib walls, they were straddling bawling calves for make-shift rodeos or trying to emulate Joe Dimaggio or Ted Williams at baseball, or competing in a softball game called "work-up." There was sledding on the ice of an overflowing water tank in the north pasture, but the most sledding fun was with their good friend and pony, Prince. A rope was tied to sled and saddle, and Prince was urged to run. During one Sunday afternoon, poor Prince was literally run into the ground. After hours of turn-taking on the sled up and down the field, by late afternoon, Prince finally just keeled over from exhaustion. After a brief respite, he was led to the barn for a reward of oats and a well-earned rest.

As more brothers followed Aelred, and later the sisters arrived, the natural spark always the precursor to chaos was doused by Mrs. Kurtenbach's strict regimen. She established rules and regulations and brought order and organization to the house. She was loving and gentle in doing it, but being nearly six feet tall, all it took for silence was the look in her eye and the shake of her finger. She seemed to them to look down on the whole world, and she demanded and got the discipline she desired of her children. She was an officious organizer. Every family chore and every function had a well -understood set of procedures, from a particular seating assignment at meals, dish washing, taking turns emptying the ubiquitous kitchen slop bucket for the hogs, or the order of use in the gradually cooling Saturday night bath water sloshing in the round tub in the kitchen. There was Mrs. Kurtenbach's way of doing it, and that's how it was done, no questions asked.

Chores, too, were assigned, explained, and given time frames for completion. And every child knew all of the farm chores and could fill in during times of illness or excused absence. Initially, when younger, the Kurtenbach children had simple household jobs like table setting, dish washing or keeping their rooms orderly and clean. As they grew older, jobs beyond the home's encircling fence-line were added to the household and farm manifest. Aelred in later life remembered all of this organization and teamwork, and many of these are lessons that are now incorporated into the employee work assignments at Daktronics, Inc.

One of the important lessons learned was the benefits of conserving energy and precious water. There never seemed enough of either to go around. Before rural electrification came to the Dimock area in the late 1940s, the family had a wind generator. When the wind blew, the charger's generator blades hummed as it sent electricity into storage in a 32-volt Delco battery system in the garage. But when the wind abated, if there had not been rules like turning lights off and conserving battery electricity in other ways, there would be no WNAX radio with the important Whitey Larson news and weather reports, the cowboy music of George B. German, or the household tips and recipes from Wynn Speece, The Neighbor Lady, whose first radio broadcast was in 1941 when Aelred was seven.

31

Not surprisingly, in the days before disposable diapers and during the droughty years of the 1930s when dirt was more common than green yard grass, Aelred's mother seemed always busy with laundry. After the clothing had dried on the clothes line, the children were called to pitch in. They dug through the clothes baskets, fishing out their own. As small children they were taught how to fold and hang each item properly. To assist them in identifying their belongings, Theodora sewed colored swatches to the insides of the items, with each child assigned a particular shape or color. The children were also expected to keep their rooms clean.

Aelred and Denis all dress up for Sunday church.

The six boys shared three of the upstairs bedrooms, two to a room, and the girls had the other, larger upstairs bedroom.

Farm chores ranged from weeding the garden and picking up corn cobs in the pig yards that could then be used as fuel for the cook stove, to feeding chickens and the other animals, or gathering eggs from beneath nest-bound, protective old hens with more cluck than pluck. There were hundreds of hay bales to stack in the barn, and to the boys, that strenuous job always seemed to come around on the hottest days of summer. Each bale weighted from sixty to seventy pounds and muscle power stacked them high to the rafters until the support posts below the haymow groaned under the stress. When the hay supply dwindled in the haymow, it freed up an ever growing space and the haymow's topography changed to a labyrinth of little alleys and dark tunnels kids and cats loved to play in. Eventually, there was space enough for the basketball hoop and backboard nailed to the west side of the barn. Spirited games of horse or half-court three-on-three were organized, with the only spectators being the nervous barn swallows who nested there.

The Kurtenbach children also walked the seemingly endless corn rows pulling or cutting down cockle burrs, sunflowers and other weedy invaders that had survived cultivation. Stones nudged from their burial beneath the field rose with the frost each year, and these, too, were hauled to field side to avoid later equipment damage. The children learned how to stack shocks of grain for drying, easy pick up and to protect them from the rain until they were loaded onto the bundle racks and taken to the threshing machine. They learned to work alone or as a team.

By the time Aelred was in the fourth grade he was regularly milking a cow, Daisy, twice a day. She remained a part of the family for about ten years. "Daisy and I became very well acquainted," he said. Over the next several years his father built the milk cow herd up until Aelred and his brothers were milking about twenty cows twice daily in the cold of winter and the stifling heat of summer, made even more uncomfortable because the doors and windows of the barn were closed to darken the milking area as a discouragement to the flies. But tails still swished over the milkers' heads and the biting, iridescent green headed flies still buzzed around them.

Aelred inspects the long abandoned milk room manger with its hand-crafted stanchions at left, where as a fourth grader, he and Daisy became close friends during the two-a-day milking sessions.

Aelred learned to milk cows before he mastered the balance of a bicycle. But in 1945 after the war when such things became available, John Kurtenbach brought a new bike home. Five rough, tough, boisterous boys learned to share that two-wheeler equally, speeding up and down the long, graveled drive way out to the mailbox and back. Because of the demand and the paces they put the bike through, it needed regular attention. Patching up that bike to race again, and exploring or working on the other mechanical marvels of the 1940s farm, were Aelred's introductions to the physics of moving mechanisms. He gained an appreciation of how they functioned and why they ceased to function. And as importantly, he learned from first-hand experience the need for regular machine maintenance.

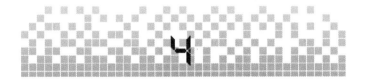

4

Daydreams and Magnetism

There is a memory of life on the farm that Aelred Kurtenbach has never forgotten: constant activity. The family arose early each day, children scurrying to dress and eat and prepare for school and for the milking and the care and feeding of the farm animals. And there is the memory of the never-ending demand to maintain and prepare the land for another year, and the need to keep farm structures repaired and useful.

"There was little time for anything else all during the school years," Kurtenbach remembered. "Our house was a hectic place, with all of the comings and goings for farming needs, for school and its functions, and for all of the other day-to-day activities of living on a farm."

When Aelred was eleven he got to drive the B John Deere tractor, and his memory of that chore doesn't include anything hectic about it at all. In fact, in his opinion, field work aboard that tractor was the most boring of any chore on a farm. He remembers the old "B" for a number of reasons beyond the monotony of it all. One is of its tobacco-stained fenders. His father

Eager for another school day, first grader Aelred, left, and Jack, a third grader.

chewed tobacco and often when driving the tractor he expectorated without sufficient power for the remains to clear the tractor fenders. "There always seemed to be a good deposit of Spark Plug there near our elbows," Aelred remembers with a smile.

Untereiner Brothers Implement in Dimock, and some of the tractors sold that day. The rubber
-tired tractor, center, was the John Deere model that Aelred learned to operate. Note the
town's water pump, center foregrond.

Plowing, not the tractor paternal patina on the fenders, was Aelred's
nemesis. He hated the job. Of all the farm chores, he considered plowing
the least enjoyable and the least creative of all. If he could have made lazy
eights or spelled out his name in plowed furrows it might have been different. But plowing was the monotonous journey up and down the field over
and over again. A startled, cackling pheasant rising before a invading tractor
wheel or a rabbit rudely rousted from an afternoon nap were very big deals
for a sleepy driver on those long hours of sameness.

"I would pull into a field of maybe forty acres with that B John Deere
and two 14-inch bottoms hooked on behind and I dreaded the coming
day," he said. "It seemed to take forever to get that field plowed." He envied
his neighbors who had wide mounted front wheels on their machines. They
could put a front tire in the furrow and the tractor would pretty much steer
itself. "They might even get out and walk beside it for exercise and a change
in scenery if they wanted to," he said. But with the B John Deere row crop
narrow front-end tractor, "you had to be up there with that steering wheel
in your hands all the time. Especially late in the day, it really turned into a
boring activity."

It was during those tedious, never-ending, back-and-forth tractor field
forays that his mind seemed always to drift to a familiar and re-occuring

daydream. During his endless journey to nowhere on that noisy old tractor, he often fantasized that he had $10,000, which he would put it in the bank to draw interest. Now foot-loose and fancy-free, he could see the world, his pretend bank account financing his fantasy trips. To travel to the four corners of the globe was his life's goal. "I wanted in the worst way to see the world," he said. "I could hardly wait." The one good part of plowing was that he had the solitude he liked, and he had time to dream of his imaginary trips to the world's most exotic places. Little did he know that in a few years, he would be visiting some of those places compliments of the United States Air Force.

Years later, as the leader of Daktronics, travel was an absolute necessity for him. On those business trips he often recalled his turns on the tractor and his daydreaming yearnings to travel. And he resolved to try to make each manufacturing task in the Daktronics process as far removed from his plowing experiences as he could. He wanted the work for each employee to be interesting, challenging, and rewarding. "Much of the so-called work ethic we hear and read about today isn't a learned ethic," he said. "People will work hard and be happy in what they are doing if each task is made interesting and challenging."

Aelred's parents finally considered him mature and strong enough to help with the heavy field work and the annual harvest that involved the use of a ponderous threshing machine. It looked like some metallic, prehistoric monster with a protruding underbelly and a giraffe-like, galvanized tin neck that directed the small grain's chaff to straw piles. During this time-honored event up through the 1940s and early 1950s, threshing machine owners took their machines from farm to farm. Helpful neighbors turned out with their teams, wagons and hayracks to assist one another. These were exciting days on the farm. The threshing machine was a mechanical wonder to Aelred. At every opportunity, including when he was allowed to watch or assist with the greasing of the gears, he explored the machine's innards, observing how the shakers and fans and all the other parts worked in concert. Another farm machine that earned his admiration was the binder that made the bundles of grain needed to satiate the threshing machine's appetite. The binder mechanism was actually able to magically tie a knot in the twine. "It made it an extremely interesting sequential machine," he explained with engineering exactness. These annual threshing days brought a joyous diversion to the usual everyday, every season sameness on the farm.

In the fall of 1940, a few months before the United States entered World War II, Aelred started first grade at Sts. Peter and Paul School in Dimock. The teachers were Benedictine Sisters from Yankton. Mother Jerome Schmidt was the Prioress of the Yankton Convent, and her younger brother, William, was the Dimock Parish Priest. The parochial schoolhouse lacked indoor plumbing, so the outhouses behind the building were kept busy, especially at recess. Aelred still remembers many of his teachers and remains appreciative of what they did to expand his horizons and to encourage him to work hard to unlock the mysteries he would discover in that little schoolhouse, which has since been razed.

Sister Marie Helene Werdel remembered Aelred. "He always had his work done and was attentive in class," she said. "All of the Kurtenbach children were well-trained at home so they knew how to help around the classroom."

Another teacher said Aelred was one of her best-ever fifth graders. "It isn't always that a teacher remembers her pupils from over sixty years ago," Sister Audrey Tramp said. "But Aelred is one that I remember as a fine young man and a good student. He came from a good home and he was very well mannered."

Aelred's first grade class shared a room with second graders, which was not uncommon in those days. He recalls that he enjoyed school from the very first day and was especially attracted to mathematics. He found science of great interest and was also an avid reader. When he was in about the fifth grade he discovered *Black Beauty* and the novels of Zane Grey, and they are still among his favorites. He did not

Jack, Aelred and Denis ready for church in 1941.

stop with Anna Sewell's only novel, or with the works of Zane Grey. He read every book he could check out from the school's library and then perused the farm magazines at his home. He also read the *Parkston Herald Advance* and *Mitchell Daily Republic* newspapers that arrived in the mailbox at the end of their long driveway leading out to the township's graveled road.

From the beginning of his schooling he showed promise as a good student. All through his eight years at Sts. Peter and Paul he more times than not was listed on the school's "A" honor roll. In a January issue of the *Herald Advance*, under the heading "Dimock News," his parents and everyone learned that first grade honor roll recipients were Sylvia Loken, James Schmidt, and Aelred Kurtenbach. Quick to catch on to concepts, his scholastic efforts were always rewarded and encouraged at home. This gave him special incentive to try even harder.

He remembers the excitement he felt the first day his teacher brought out automobile magneto magnets to be put through their magical paces interacting with metal filings. It was probably at that time that he decided he would study electricity when he was older. He was from that time on captivated by the mysteries of electricity. At every opportunity he tried to learn more about it. "Those old magnets impressed my youthful curiosity greatly, and probably set my future course more than anything else," he remembered.

A quiet boy with a tendency toward bashfulness, he got a much-needed boost to his self-esteem in the seventh grade. He was given the honor of reading the Passion according to St. Matthew on Palm Sunday, now known as Passion

Aelred at confirmation as a fifth grader.

Sunday, before Easter. He had a few days to prepare, and he practiced and practiced. When Palm Sunday arrived, he carried the Bible with him to the choir loft of the church, but he had memorized the fairly long passage front to back so well that he never once had to glance down for a reminder of the text.

Another of his joys was watching and learning as his father managed the farm, and in particular, excelled in the marketing of his hogs.

The Kurtenbach farm, while diversified, specialized mostly in raising hogs. Aelred especially enjoyed working with pigs and the farrowing process. "I considered hogs as the economic generator for our farm," he remembered. "Dad was a good, efficient, knowledgeable pork producer." He admired his father's particular talent for raising hogs, historically referred to as "mortgage lifters" by farmers. John Kurtenbach had a way of sorting through the proclivities of the market, and Aelred learned from that and he, too, tried to follow the market reports published in the newspapers. His father seemed always a step ahead, anticipating what the market might bring the next day or the next week.

The Kurtenbachs also raised cattle, but not to the extent of the Kurtenbach hog operation. Not all the pigs or steers went to market. A few were sacrificed for the good of the Kurtenbach table. A prime steer, bawling and stomping nervously in the farm trailer, was hauled to Parkston for butchering, but the hogs were processed on the farm. Neighbors often helped one another in the butchering season. At the Kutenbach farm, three hogs in the

Hogs were usually the money makers on the Kurtenbach farm.

200-pound range would be slaughtered, then cleaned and scalded in a barrel of boiling water to help in the removal of the hair. The carcass was then halved.

The halves were taken inside the Kurtenbach washroom for further butchering. "It was quite a sight to see six hog halves lined up on our extended kitchen table moved from the kitchen out into the wash room," Aelred remembered. The children helped, taking turns grinding meat for sausage made according to old German ways. Each batch was combined with a modicum of beef and some spices to give it color and a zesty taste. The children also helped stuff the mixture into sausage casings. The sausage was then baked, cut into shorter lengths, and placed in two-quart Mason jars. Melted lard was poured over the meat for an airtight seal and safe storage in the basement. "It was absolutely delicious," Aelred remembered. "We enjoyed eating it and we also had fun putting it up."

In 1940, Aelred's father bought a new two-door Plymouth. It was destined to became legendary with the Kurtenbach boys. But initially, it was the sedate family car. It carried the Kurtenbach entrourage to school, church, and to Saturday nights of shopping, fun, and socializing in Dimock or Parkston. Starting out on any of these occasions, with a typical German need for order, there was a proper plan for entering and for sitting in the car. Aelred, Jack, and Denis got in first and sat in the back seat. Three more younger Kutenbachs, DeWayne, Eva, and Frank, then squeezed in and sat on their laps. Depending on the year, there could be three babies or smaller children in the front seat with Mr. and Mrs. Kurtenbach.

Saturday night excursions to town in the 1930s and 1940s were the events of the week, a time to leave the drudgery and monotony of rural isolation behind and head for the bright lights. Farm families combined business and pleasure, meeting old friends and comparing farming notes and news. Retired farmers and their wives, and everyone else living in town, also joined the main street festivities. Children headed out to explore stores and streets. Mothers shopped and fathers dropped off the cream and eggs at the cooperative and then joined their fellow farmers to catch up on county and area news. The visiting and the enterprise extended far into the evening.

On a Saturday night trip to Dimock in the spring of 1942, Aelred and his family learned of the new twenty-ton scale just installed in the Farmers

Grain Elevator and Stock Company that hugged the railroad track on the east side of town. They marveled in late 1941 when the town turned on its few newly installed streetlights. Kids peeked into the fire hall to see Dimock's big red fire truck that everyone lovingly called "Jerky John."

When the family drove to Parkston on Saturday nights, each child was handed as much as a quarter in mad money, the amount probably depending on the price of hogs that week. Some of that hog money may have been spent at Lawrence Schlimgen's little popcorn stand on the south side of Main Street. That left plenty of cash for a candy bar or an ice cream cone at Koehn's or Schilling's Grocery Store. Later, when the boys were older, some of the money might have also been spent on haircuts at Earl Grey's Barber Shop. (But the boys when younger got haircuts from their parents and then learned how to cut one another's hair reasonably well. It was discovered that little brother Frank had a particular talent for the job and he soon became the Kurtenbach family expert at giving his brothers their "flat top" haircuts.)

A regular stop in Parkston was at Bill Fix's shoe repair shop. Shoes in the Kurtenbach family wore out with alacrity. They were repaired and handed down from one child to another. There was always need for shoe repair, and besides, Mr. Fix was an especially close friend of John Kurtenbach.

Saturday nights in town were bonanzas for local businesses. A front page

Parkston's main street as it appeared when Aelred was growing up. The Alvero Theater at right was where he saw his first motion picture at age 12.

item in the *Parkston Advance* in June 1942 reminded Parkston residents not to park their cars downtown on Saturday nights in order "to make room for those who wish to patronize Parkston from out of town." Further, it urged businesses to keep their establishments and the city sidewalks clean for the visitors. Trash was to be swept into a pile in front of their place of business and "city trucks would be around on Saturday morning to haul it away."

It was on a very special Sunday afternoon in Parkston, with his parents' blessing, that Aelred, when he was twelve, saw his first motion picture. It was at the Alvero Theater, named for its auctioneer owner Al Wuebben and his wife Veronica. Starring in the movie *Going My Way* were Bing Crosby and Barry Fitzgerald, who played the part of Catholic priests. Aelred remembers the admission price was twelve cents, so he also had change enough from his quarter for a big bag of theater popcorn. Often, the price of a movie at the Alvero during the depression was a live chicken. One clucking old hen would get the whole family into the show.

The quarter for town on Saturday nights was often augmented by money the boys earned when they were older working at odd jobs for area farmers. One summer, the boys formed what could be called the Kurtenbach Cooperative Bank. Whatever money any of them earned was put into a coffee can, and each week the boys each drew out an equal amount of spending money. "We all trusted one another and it worked remarkably well," remembered Aelred.

As the children grew older, there just wasn't room enough in the Plymouth for everyone. So two trips to the church were necessary to get everyone there, or church was a two-mass affair. The Kurtenbachs attended church in shifts.

In the fall of 1949, with Jack and Aelred attending high school in Parkston, they inherited the trusty Plymouth and their parents purchased a roomy 1950 Packard. After Jack graduated in 1950 and Aelred became a senior in the fall of 1951, he was one of four Kurtenbach brothers roaming the hallways, one for every grade down to Frank the freshman. So all year long on weekdays like clockwork, the Plymouth rumbled into Parkston spewing a roiling wake of faint blue exhaust smoke, with the four strapping Kurtenbach boys aboard headed for classes. The Plymouth was a familiar, recognizable sight in northern Hutchinson County. After chores were finished in the evenings and on the weekends, the car carried the boys back to Parkston for school functions, ballgames, and occasional night time rabbit hunts.

The old dinged up Plymouth was also called upon for truck-

The Kurtenbach family car was a 1950 Packard, that with planning, could transport all of the Kurtenbach children to town and church.

ing duty. It was the boys' responsibility to take milk from the farm to the Dimock Cheese Factory. The milk, in ten-gallon cans, was carefully placed in the car's trunk for that regular trip to the Dimock plant.

The old car, with big fenders for hunters to sit on, was perfect for rabbit hunts that provided popular sport for the Kurtenbach boys. Rabbits were inundating South Dakota in those days and were considered destructive pests. The Sts. Peter and Paul Ladies Altar Society often teamed with men of the parish in sponsoring rabbit hunts. Money raised helped with worthy church projects. During the especially snow-bound February 1940, deep snow covered the usual rabbit delicacies. So jackrabbits and cottontails nibbled on the only available fare, the not-so-delicious but nutritious bark of trees with trunks no bigger than broom handles that were just getting started in new farm shelterbelts, a conservation practice spurred on by the soil losses during the long 1930s drought.

The U.S. Forest Service encouraged rabbit hunts to protect their tree investments shared on a matching basis with farmers. During that February alone, after seven organized hunts in the Dimock area, 925 tree-nibbling rabbits were shot and sold to mink ranchers. After the hunts, the ladies served free lunch in the church community center. As an added incentive and a "thank you" for the donated cash from the hunt, they also awarded each hunter one shotgun shell for each rabbit bagged.

The hither and yon trips in the busy old Plymouth, often seen barreling down Hutchinson County gravel roads spewing dust ditch to ditch, required plenty of gas. Fortunately for the boys, their father kept a big storage

Comprising two-thirds of a baseball team, the Kurtenbach brothers prepare to depart for a Sunday afternoon pick-up game in the Dimock area, from left Jack, Frank, Ivan, Aelred, Denis and DeWayne. The old Plymouth car filled with Kurtenbach boys was a common sight in Hutchinson County.

tank of it on the farm for his machinery. It was free for the taking when their father wasn't close by, Aelred joked. Strangely, the big tank's gauge often was rendered inoperable when certain wires mysteriously "broke loose" from the measuring mechanism. So no one really ever knew how much gasoline had been removed before the coop gas truck came by each week to top it off again.

When the Plymouth wheezed its last, regurgitating a piston rod, the car was left idle in a farmyard purgatory. Most boys would be tempted to dig right in to the motor to see how it worked, but Aelred's electrical curiosities centered on the dashboard. "I was interested in the instrumentation and the electrical controls," he remembered.

The Kurtenbach boys were all good athletes and they inherited their mother's size. Aelred was the smallest of the six boys. Frank, the barber, was the biggest and the most athletic. Aelred found sports enjoyable and also had other interests. One was membership in the Parkston Future Farmers of America chapter. Basketball was not his forte, but when his FFA chapter played the Geddes FFA chapter, Aelred's team won 38-34, and Aelred was game high point man with eighteen points.

Aelred's farm chores prevented him from going out for football except

45

during his senior year. The Parkston Trojans football team had insufficient weight and heft in the line. So after the season's first two football game in the fall of 1951, Trojan football coach Floyd Mitchell drove out to talk to John Kurtenbach. He inquired if 190-pound Aelred and his younger brother, 205-pound DeWayne, could join the team as tackles and play in the game against the Platte Black Panthers. John gave his approval.

Aelred Kurtenbach, number 34 on the 1951 Parkston High School football team.

Daily farm chores still had to be done, so Aelred and his younger brother Denis, a junior, worked out an interesting agreement. If Denis would assume the chores assigned to Aelred that year so Aelred could participate in sports, Aelred promised to stay home for one year after high school graduation and do the chores assigned to Denis, and he could then participate in sports his senior year.

Spring and summer storms often brought farm work to a halt. Tornados could ruin a farm, and many farms had storm cellars underground and away from the house. Those without that protection sought refuge in the basement if tornados were seen or predicted. At the Kurtenbach home, protection from the threat of tornadoes was prayer. At anytime during the day, or the middle of the night, if storm clouds gathered, Mrs. Kurtenbach called her children into the living room to pray mightily for the Lord's intercession while the wind blew and the rain pounded on the roof.

The infamous Thanksgiving blizzard of 1948, the blustery worst of the decade, stopped Hutchinson County and most of eastern South Dakota in their tracks. Thursday, November 18, blew in cold. Snow began to fall. By Friday, Nov. 19, the wind increased to a howling crescendo. The weight of nearly ten inches of snow driven by winds in excess of fifty miles an hour caused roofs to collapse. Vehicles, including trains, were stranded in drifts that might be blocks long and tree high. Livestock was stranded in fields

The end of another school day at Parkston High School as most of the students board buses for rides to their farm homes.

and feed lots, drifting with the wind into fenced corners where many suffocated in deep snow drifts. Near Madison, north and east of Dimock, a farmer went out to shoo his chickens to safety. He became disoriented in the driving snow and never returned to the house. Snow in Dimock drifted ten feet deep into sheltered spots, then was packed concrete hard by the high winds.

For Parkston High School freshman Aelred Kurtenbach, it was not only a vicious Dakota blizzard, it became a life-changing storm, setting his future course. Aelred and his older brother Jack rode the school bus to Parkston High School as usual on Thursday morning, and the other Kurtenbach children were driven to class at Sts. Peter and Paul School in Dimock.

By 2 p.m. Thursday, the seriousness of the storm was becoming evident. "We'd just completed the cross county season and were turning in our gear when we were told that the school buses were not going to be operating," Kurtenbach said. Homes in Parkston were found for all of the country kids there, and the children in Sts. Peter and Paul School in Dimock stayed overnight at the school. Aelred and his older brother were told to go to the home of their aunt and uncle, Christine and John Bowar, who lived a few blocks from the school. All that night the wind howled and the snow scratched at the doors and windows of houses all over southeastern South Dakota.

On Saturday it had let up some. The Parkston to Dimock rail line was cleared. Aelred, Jack, and other Dimock-area children were rounded up by Parkston school officials and crowded into the freight train's caboose because there were no passenger cars available. Most of the children had never ridden on a train, let alone in the caboose, so for all the youngsters it was an enjoyable six-mile excursion to the Dimock depot. (The Depot, by the way, is now an historic display at the Sons of the Middle Border Museum in nearby Mitchell.)

Snow had drifted, closing the Kurtenbach driveway and the country road from house to town. So John, as he had before Aelred's birth fourteen years before, hitched Barney and Chub (King had since retired) to the wagon. He threw on a pitchfork or two of hay for comfort. Mrs. Kurtenbach carried out warm blankets and extra coats to add to the load. John slapped the reins, and the horses started for Dimock to rescue his younger children from the Catholic school there, and to wait at the depot to meet Jack and Aelred.

By the time they all arrived back home it was early evening, and chores were waiting. The cows came first. They hadn't been milked on their regular schedule. Passageways to all of the outbuildings had to be chopped out and shoveled free. "At that time people didn't have snowblowers or snowplows or any snow handling equipment," It was all done with shovels. "It was also a challenge to get the milk cows back on a milking schedule and to keep them from contracting udder infections because of the schedule disruption," he remembered.

The blizzard gradually abated by Saturday night, but roads were still blocked and there was considerable work to do to get the farm back to normalcy. It seemed an impossible task under trying conditions. As he worked, Aelred got it into his head that he should forego school for the rest of the school year. He would stay at home to help his father, then 58. School resumed the next Tuesday, but Aelred stayed home to help. And all that week, working twelve to fifteen hours a day, he became even more convinced that it would be too much work for his father to handle alone. The blizzard had also cost the family some much-needed money. The Sioux Falls Stockyard hog market that week lost $1.25, dropping to $21.25 per hundred pounds for hogs.

Aelred dearly loved school and the challenge of study, and he wanted desperately to return to complete his freshman year. But for the good of the family and the farm, he talked with his parents about the possibility of dropping out of school. John and Theodora were consumed with extra work because of the blizzard, and for a time considered that possibility, too. But as they thought about it, they decided that Aelred should resume his school work. Aelred remembers that his father, who hadn't finished grade school because of childhood illnesses, discouraged him from becoming a farmer. The "next year" philosophy of the farmer rarely held true. "He encouraged me to find something else to do. He said there were better ways to make a living than to be a farmer. He was a frustrated farmer, and he didn't want me to end up as one, too."

Somehow, the farm would survive, his father told him. So Aelred returned to school. "It was one of those decisions that was a correct decision and it had a great impact on my life." When he returned to classes, he seemed even more intent on doing well in his studies.

Aelred's high school days passed by quickly, it seemed to him. As was the custom, the school newspaper interviewed all seniors. The interview with Aelred, the blond young man with a quiet, courteous demeanor, was brief and his interview hinted of his reticence. All that the reporter could pry from the tight-lipped Aelred were six brief lines. He "likes sirloin steaks and the song 'Slow Poke'." His favorite pastimes were "sports and movies." His proudest moment, he said, was "the day he learned how to throw the

Aelred Kurtenbach's high school graduation picture, 1952.

49

shot put in track practice."

And his future plans?

"Indefinite," was his response.

And they were.

He still owed his brother Denis a year's worth of farm chores. And while milking, pitching hay, and cultivating with the old "B" tractor, he'd have plenty of time to think about traveling the world and what he would do with his life.

He didn't know it at the time, but those old automobile magnetos that performed the unbelievable magic on the little metal filings in grade school science class, and the configurations of the dials and meters would have much to do with what was in store for him.

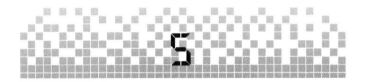

New Horizons

Aelred Kurtenbach doesn't consider his year of full-time farming after high school as a year of penance, his cost for that final uninterrupted season of Parkston High School sports. He'd traded off chores with his younger brother so Denis could concentrate on sports without the farm duties that would infringe on football practices and games. Kurtenbach remembers his year after high school working on the family farm as a time to relax, enjoy this brief period in his life when he could work at his own pace, and to get to know his parents better.

"I even had time to read the newspapers and fix things up around the farm, and I especially enjoyed the opportunity it gave me to spend time with my parents, visiting with them as an adult about their philosophies of life and other subjects that I hadn't considered or thought about earlier in my life," he said.

He relished the quietude of full-time farming and welcomed the rigid schedule that farming requires. Working with his father made it even more rewarding. And, of course, he was pleased that he could return a favor to his brother, making it possible for Denis to concentrate on sports as Aelred had been able to do the previous year.

"It was an interesting and reflective year for me because I finally had some free time and a much less hectic schedule," Kurtenbach said. While his classmates were leaving for college or beginning careers elsewhere, Kurten-

Aelred's father, John, with second youngest son Frank, now a Daktronics official.

bach spent the remaining months of 1952 after graduation as a full-time farmer.

Some of what Kurtenbach was reading about in the local papers was related to the Korean War and the young men from Hutchinson County who were leaving, either by choice or because of the national draft, to serve their country during this time of need. Occasionally, the news saddened the Kurtenbach family and all of the community.

Everyone read about Sgt. Clement J. Schlimgen, a fellow member of Sts. Peter and Paul Church in Dimock who was eight years older than Aelred. Schlimgen was wounded in action in Korea on September 4, 1951. He died later in the year. The soldier's funeral was held Nov. 27, 1951, at Sts. Peter and Paul Church with the Parkston Guard of Honor attending.

News of the Korean conflict had Aelred and his lifelong friend Herb Wermers discussing the war and how it might influence their future. They concluded that they would soon be prime candidates for the Hutchinson County draft quota and decided that they should enlist before being called by the Hutchinson County Draft Board. That way, they could better control their destiny. The Air Force and the Navy seemed their best options because, the young men reasoned, those two branches appeared to offer more educational opportunities.

Their final choice was the Air Force. After enlisting at Mitchell, they rode with their parents in early January of 1953 to Sioux Falls where they met up with about a dozen other new Air Force recruits from South Dakota for physical examinations, the swearing in ceremony, and the long train ride to Air Force boot camp. Kurtenbach's odyssey, so arduously planned and worked out in his mind while driving the tractor on the Dimock farm, had now been launched. His dream of being a wayfaring vagabond had finally materialized, albeit not with $10,000 in the bank to finance his exotic sojourns to the world's vacation spots, but with a extra few dollars his father had slipped into his hand during family goodbyes before leaving for San Antonio, Texas, thirty hours from South Dakota.

Ahead for Kurtenbach and Wermers were three months of basic training at Lackland Air Force Base. Even though the next few years of new places, new experiences, and educational opportunities were unknown and unplanned at the time, they would, ironically, fit perfectly into the early experiences of a man who would one day launch an international business.

The Air Force way wasn't exactly what Kurtenbach expected. On the farm, the family had worked in a collaborative manner. Each member of the family had certain chores accomplished with an understanding of how and, most importantly, why they were done. "The military life was different," Kurtenbach remembered. "I didn't always understand why things were being done as they were, and I felt the various instructors in basic training didn't focus enough on the 'why' of it."

But Kurtenbach soon adjusted to this lifestyle change, and he quickly adapted to the Air Force way. He now looks back upon his military experiences as having a positive influence on his life. The Air Force and the other services are arguably the world's best in conducting vocational and aptitude testing, and in Kurtenbach's case, his knowledge and interest in electronics quickly became apparent.

He was selected to attend the Air Force's technical school in electronics at Biloxi, Mississippi, where he would begin training as either a radar or a radio technician. While thrilled with the opportunity to be training and eventually working in a field he thoroughly enjoyed, it meant that he and his good Dimock friend would be parting ways. Wermers became a radio technician, but via another route.

The six-month electronics training course was at Keesler Air Force Base in Biloxi. It took place in the pre-transistor era, so Kurtenbach and the other eager young airmen became proficient and knowledgeable with vacuum tubes, capacitors, resistors, inductors, and other passive components that are now practically museum pieces.

Because the Korean War meant that a large number of Air Force personnel had to be enrolled in the courses, and the need for small class sizes because of the technicalities involved, the school's classes were held in four six-hour shifts. Kurtenbach attended classes in the evening, and that suited him.

The remainder of his time was spent studying and in recreational pursuits, including a healthy dose of sporting events and an occasional visit to the base canteen. Kurtenbach completed the difficult course with ease. Because of high marks and a natural interest in the field of electronics that impressed his instructors, he was asked to take an advanced eight-week program. In that school, the regimen allowed time for excursions to nearby New Orleans, where Kurtenbach especially enjoyed the jazz music blaring from practically every Bourbon Street bistro and taproom. He's still an avid jazz fan.

After the sights and sounds of the French Quarter and New Orleans in general, it was back to the grind, learning the proper hands-on procedures in the care and feeding of radar, as well as surviving the long lectures in hot, stuffy classrooms. When Kurtenbach completed his training in mid-November of 1954, he learned he would be assigned to duty in Japan.

Before leaving for the Land of the Rising Sun in January of 1955 he had a welcome 45-day leave that enabled him to spend Thanksgiving and Christmas back home. As an added bonus, he arrived in Hutchinson County just in time to enjoy the joyous camaraderie of pheasant hunting with some of his brothers. Of course, they also joined in on various evening activities in and around the Parkston and Mitchell areas, including a party

the day before his leave ended on January 3. So he was able to celebrate his departure for duty as well as his twenty-first birthday.

A bleary-eyed Kurtenbach was up early the next morning. His parents drove him to Columbus, Nebraska, where he boarded a Union Pacific passenger train bound for San Francisco. There, he and others awaited processing and surface transportation across the Pacific to their new duty station in Japan. A ship for the two-week cruise was due in a few days, allowing time for Kurtenbach to experience and explore San Francisco.

His assignment in the Far East wasn't exactly how he'd planned it all out. While in radar school, he had so impressed his instructors with his

Aelred working on the radar site during his Air Force service in Japan.

skill, knowledge, and talent in electronics that he was offered the opportunity to remain at the school as an instructor. But Kurtenbach still had that B John Deere tractor-inspired urge to travel and to experience other cultures. He said that he preferred to be assigned duty in Europe, reasoning that perhaps travel could take him to some of his forefathers' home areas in Germany. But with typical military rationale, he was promptly sent in exactly the opposite direction: to the Far East.

The day to board ship soon arrived, and he found a bunk on a vintage WW II troop ship for the wallowing ride to Osaka, Japan. Long, chilly days were spent at gin rummy, books, and boredom. The ship tied up at Yokuska, the famous war-time Japanese military base and sea port, and Kurtenbach and others in the Air Force contingent were bused to Tachikawa Air Force Base sixteen miles west of Tokyo.

On his first night ashore, Kurtenbach and other curious airmen toured the night life and the sights and sounds of downtown Tachikawa. On the bus with the other wide-eyed GI's, Kurtenbach was surprised when Bill Fix, Jr., in typical "it's a small world" fashion, tapped him on the shoulder. Bill's father was the shoemaker friend of Kurtbenbach's father, back in Parkston. Kurtenbach's other memories of that first evening in Japan include the proliferation of busy, scurrying people everywhere, and the bright panoply of flashing neon signs that turned night to day.

After a few days laying around in a stuffy Air Force barracks on the Tachikawa Air Base, Private First Class Kurtenbach boarded a crowded train for the town of Hitachi, a rail center about ninety miles from Tokyo. An airman at the station there flagged him down and drove him in a bouncing Jeep to his new post, a former Japanese radar site near the small village of Omika, about two or three miles from Japan's east coast. Less than a decade before, radar signals for the Omika site were beaming east over the Pacific to warn Japan's air defenses of the approaching B-17 and B-24 bombers. The site was eventually destroyed by shellings from U. S. Navy ships near the end of WWII .

Now, having been rebuilt by the U. S. Air Force, the site was equipped with the Signal Corps Radio 239 radar set (SCR), a system first used in 1939 and considered antiquated, although it sufficed at measuring distances and was able to detect aircraft approximately 135 miles out. The radar site and camp were somewhat primitive, considering that WW II had ended eight years earlier. The living units for the approximately sixty airmen were tents that had wooden floors and wooden frames, with the canvas stretched over the roofs and walls. The walls could be rolled up for ventilation during the warmer months. The camp also had a few Quonset huts, including one for the administrative branch of the small base, and another used as a recreational building and a PX club. The site would be Kurtenbach's home for the next eight months.

The large contingent of radar maintenance technicians at the site meant that Kurtenbach and the others would have an abundance of free time for other pursuits. Each technician worked regular eight-hour shifts. But because there were so many technicians, most nights were free. So with plenty of "off time," Kurtenbach and the others settled in on various time-killing pursuits, such as card games, letter writing, travel excursions, reading books, attending an occasional movie at the base's tented theater, or playing basketball at a nearby school. In the warmer months, there was baseball and softball interspersed with time at the beach. Kurtenbach had never had a real vacation, and he considered his summer in Japan as the next best thing, compliments of the Air Force.

In hindsight, he also remembered his summer of 1955 in Japan was an educational and an enjoyable experience. He made new friends, among them Howard Nagano, a first generation Japanese, and John Lukechevitz, with whom Kurtenbach still maintains contact. Lukechevitz, like Kurtenbach, chose electrical engineering as his life's work.

As summer's fun in the sun wound down, a request came to the Omika radar site for two radar maintenance technicians at an Air Force radar station in Okinawa. Kurtenbach and two of his friends expressed interest. "We drew straws to see who would be reassigned, and I lost," Kurtenbach remembered. Years later, when Kurtenbach's new company, Daktronics, was working with another new business in Brookings, Falcon Industries, he and Falcon founder Don Bender compared Air Force notes. To their surprise, they discovered that Bender had been stationed at the Okinawa radar site and remembered when the two Omika radar technicians transferred into his station.

In early Fall of 1955, another request for an Omika station radar technician arrived from headquarters. This time the need was in Korea. No straws were drawn. Kurtenbach was it. The aircraft that took him to the war-torn country landed at the Seoul Airport outside South Korea's capitol city. There, Kurtenbach learned that he would be assigned to a base known only as K-6. It was a small base for fighter aircraft, but it had fairly significant radar, including long range radar to detect enemy aircraft, mainly the swift and shifty MIG jet fighters that were commonly used by the Chinese and North Koreans during the Korean conflict that was just winding down by the time Kurtenbach arrived on the peninsula.

Aelred at the K-6 radar station in Korea.

Although MIG aircraft incursions into South Korean air space were few, Kurtenbach remembers several exciting days when his radar-mates picked up blips from the north and alerted K-6 pilots, who scrambled to chase the enemy fighters back north of the 38th parallel. Returning to K-6 after the confrontations, American pilots enjoyed putting their F-80 Sabre jets through their paces, performing low victory rolls over the base to release some of their battle-tension and to let everyone know that their mission had been successfully accomplished.

Kurtenbach settled in at K-6 for an eight-month stay that would bring him to the end of his two-year obligation for Far East service. He spent his time studying the details of the Bendix, RCA and General Electric radar, working with other airmen and with company technicians and engineers who were there. He welcomed the opportunity to learn more about everything electronic. So impressed were those responsible for the radar and its maintenance that within two months after he arrived at K-6 Kurtenbach was named the non-commissioned officer in charge of the all non-commissioned enlisted members of Air Force radar maintenance group there. "This was a real morale boost for me, and also gave me the opportunity to gain leadership experience and experience in managing people," he remembered. Later, he was recognized as Airman of the Month for his attention to detail and skill at his job.

As in Japan, there were also opportunities at K-6 for participation in sports. Football was the "touch" variety, which was often a rather loose term for "do what you can to win." With bored, energetic young men at play, it could easily evolve into a contact sport, and Kurtenbach has the teeth to prove it. As he had in high school, he played in the line, and that's where he took an unexpected and untimely punch to the mouth. Two of his front teeth were knocked loose. Fortunately, his coach was also the base dentist, and he quickly managed to anchor them back in place.

As the numbing cold of the Korean autumn set in, the basketball season started. A spare quonset hut was converted to a makeshift court and games only slightly less physically demanding than the so-called "touch" football started. Hunting, too, was a popular but unproductive pastime. Kurtenbach and others were out before sunup in quest of the migrating honkers and squawking ducks they could hear overhead. But goose and duck hunting in Korea proved more difficult than the forays Kurtenbach remembered experiencing in South Dakota. "We never did kill a duck or a goose," he admitted.

Days drifted by during the cold peninsula winter, and Friday, April 13, 1956, wasn't at all an unlucky day for Kurtenbach. It was in fact a rather joyous one. He received his orders to report "stateside" to Tinker Air Force Base near Oklahoma City. Better still, he also received a thirty-day leave, and for even more frosting on the cake, he was scheduled to fly back to the United States, rather than bounce back on a slow boat. The military plane, after a brief refueling stop in Japan, banked east toward Oakland, California. Once there, after routine processing, Kurtenbach boarded a commercial flight to Omaha, Nebraska, and from there to South Dakota where his father met him at the Mitchell Airport. "It was great to be home again," he remembered. "I didn't realize how much I had missed my dad and all of my family until I got home."

It was while he was enjoying his time back at the farm and socializing at familiar haunts and watering holes that Kurtenbach—with money saved while overseas—invested in a six-year-old Plymouth. At the time, he didn't realize what a faithful, long-time partner that old car would become. It would transport him to many new places and new adventures. After his leave ended, he and his "new" car headed to Sweetwater, Texas, where in the interim of his leave, he had been reassigned from Tinker Air Force Base. He would continue his radar servicing work at the Sweetwater Radar Station until his enlistment ended and he was honorably discharged in November of 1957.

As in Japan and Korea, administrators at the Sweetwater site quickly recognized Kurtenbach's expertise and knowledge of the range finding FPS3 and the height finding radar FPS6. He was made a crew chief for the first several months, and then—as he had been in Korea—he was placed in charge of all of the enlisted personnel responsible for radar maintenance at Sweetwater. It was an honor, and he again appreciated the opportunity to further hone his leadership skills. Under Kurtenbach's watch, the Sweetwater radar site was repeatedly judged among the best maintained in the Air Force's Central Defense Command.

Kurtenbach not only became even more of an expert in radar maintenance while at Sweetwater, but he also acquired another unique skill. He became a bartender. It was his night job—three nights a week—at the base NCO club. Of course, he also continued to participate in sports and—as he has continued to do all of his life—decided to try something new and different. At Sweetwater, he took up tennis, a sport he continues to dabble in, although he readily admits he's not quite ready for prime time.

While working, bartending, learning the backhand on the courts, and realizing that the next phase of his life was nearly upon him, Kurtenbach began to consider what his future would be. He thought about going back to farming in Dimock, but remembered his father's advice and frustration. So instead of farming, Kurtenbach decided to capitalize on his interest and knowledge of radar and electronics. He would pursue a college degree in electrical engineering. He explored engineering colleges, narrowing his choice to three, including nearby Texas Tech and the two engineering colleges in South Dakota. The school quarter at the School of Mines and Technology at Rapid City was scheduled to begin after Thanksgiving that year, 1957. He applied to the Air Force for an early discharge to enable him to enroll before the school's second quarter, and to his surprise his request was granted.

The timing of his early release couldn't have been more propitious. He was able to spend time back home helping his brother DeWayne, recently discharged from the Navy, and his parents prepare for the sale of their farm. At that time, incidentally, three of their siblings—Denis, Eva, and Frank—were all enrolled at South Dakota State University in Brookings. After the farm sale and helping his parents move into a new home they had built in Parkston, Kurtenbach and his faithful 1950 Plymouth headed west to Rapid City, the School of Mines and Technology, and his next adventure.

His first measure of good luck at the School of Mines was being assigned a dormitory roommate named Ken Yocum. Yocum would eventually became an instructor of mathematics at South Dakota State University, and later head of the Math Department there, so the two former college roommates were destined to became fellow faculty members at the state Land Grant institution.

Kurtenbach naturally gravitated to other former service members enrolled at the school, all older freshman. "We became a tight-knit group of good friends, supporting and helping one another," he remembered. Kurtenbach remains in contact with two of the "old timers," Keith Messer, in Minneapolis, and Reece Palmer, who is now also retired and living in Oklahoma. Having missed the first quarter of school that year, Kurtenbach enrolled in summer school, catching up in math, chemistry, and English. By the time classes started in the Fall of 1958 he was a true college sophomore.

During the summer, in between classes, Kurtenbach found a part-time job in a television shop in Rapid City repairing sets. He continued working after class

Aelred, home from college for a pheasant hunt.

and on weekends until December 1958. At that time he also decided there should be more to college than work and study. He become more involved in some extracurricular, out-of-class opportunities. He dove right in to the school and the community social scenes. He tried athletics and became involved in student politics. He also immersed himself in other student activities. The bashful, somewhat reticent farm kid from Parkston High School was emerging from his shell.

He and Reece Palmer joined Theta Tau, the engineering fraternity. This would eventually steer him into student politics. Another new experience for Kurtenbach was collegiate wrestling. At the urging of his younger brother Frank, who was making a name for himself as a championship heavyweight wrestler at South Dakota State University (SDSU), he decided he'd try out for the sport at the School of Mines. He also became acquainted with SDSU's wrestling coach Warren Williamson, and this proved to be a long-lasting friendship. Neither knew it at the time, but their friendship would eventually result in the creation of the first successful scoreboard exclusively for wrestling that Kurtenbach's company would develop.

Kurtenbach soon learned that wrestling team practices and workouts under the watchful eye his wresting coach, Homer Englund, who was also the school's football coach, required long hours and the difficult regimine of maintaining weight, both of which Kurtenbach learned were easier said than done. But he'd always liked to be challenged in whatever he did, and he set his chin straight for the long haul on the wrestling mat. He lost thirty pounds in order to make the Hardrocker team at 175 pounds. He enjoyed the sport, but admits he wasn't destined for an Olympic team tryout. "I think I only was victorious in one or two matches during the year and a half that I competed," he recalled. "However, wrestling was good for me. It helped me lose weight and really developed a discipline on maintaining weight control and on completing what I started."

His experience in the sport would also help later when his firm developed the first scoreboard designed for wrestling. "I remembered that when I wrestled, it was difficult to look up to the basketball scoreboard to learn how much time was left in the match," he said. The Daktronics scoreboard developed ten years later was designed for mat-side use and was much easier to see for the fans and the wrestlers.

Another new collegiate experience for Kurtenbach was becoming a member of the Newman Club, a Catholic student organization. He never regretted the decision to join, because that's where he met Irene McDonell, his future wife. The School of Mines, then with a student body comprised almost exclusively of young men, combined its Newman Club activities with a contingent from the National College of Business in Rapid City. It was after the club's Janaury 1959 meeting that a number in the group decided to visit a local pub and collegiate hangout known as Angelo's.

And that's where Kurtenbach met Irene. Like Kurtenbach, she was from a small South Dakota town, Murdo, graduating from high school there in 1957. She was studying secretarial science. During the evening at Angelo's, they discovered they had many similar interests. They both enjoyed dancing, and Kurtenbach, still somewhat shy and reserved, found Irene easy to talk to and to be with. A week later Kurtenbach had worked up nerve enough to call her for a date. She accepted, and in his faithful old Plymouth, the car that had never failed him, they drove out to a popular drive-in theater in East Rapid. After the movie—neither Kurtenbach or Irene now remember the film's title—while driving back to town, the Plymouth coughed, sputtered, and stopped. Kurtenbach left his somewhat irritated first date alone in the car and hiked back to a service station for a container of gasoline. "Somehow she managed to forgive me for that inconvenience and we continued to date," Kurtenbach remembered.

As if the demands of the Hardrocker wrestling team, Newman Club, collegiate football, working his way through a difficult academic regimen, and courting Irene McDonell weren't enough, Kurtenbach waded in to another demanding activity. At the urging of his fraternity brothers, and with their work and support, he ran for and was elected to the school's student governing body, the Board of Control. He served on that prestigious board for two years, the final one as Student Body president. "My fraternity brothers did a good job of managing my campaign," he said. He doesn't recall now what his vote-getting campaign promises to School of Mines students were, but "I probably campaigned on the old standby of better food in the student cafeteria and on the need for improvement of the roads through the married student housing area."

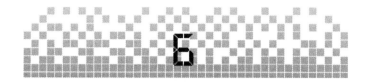

A Partnership Formed

The summer of 1959, back in Parkston to earn money to supplement his monthly GI Bill check of $110 that single military veterans attending school received, Kurtenbach was hired by the Freeman Cooperative in Freeman, South Dakota, working five days a week, starting at 4:30 a.m. His job was driving a truck and picking up cream and eggs on a different route radiating out from Freeman each day. "It was nice to be able to see the people, many whom I had known all my life," he said. "But because of the long days on the routes I was still very happy when the summer break was over. I looked forward to getting back to college."

Undoubtedly, seeing Irene again was also a part of his agenda for that school year. He packed the 1950 Plymouth and headed for the Hardrocker Fall Football Camp. Three games into the 1959 season he earned a starting center spot, tenuous front teeth from Korean football and gimpy knee from a Dimock badger hole and all. He had a wonderful time with great teammates, and he'll forever remember the highlight of his collegiate gridiron career: defeating rival Northern State University on that school's homecoming, Gypsy Day. "It was Northern's only loss of the year," he remembered. It's still a game dissected and replayed at every Class of 1961 School of Mines reunion.

After a Christmas break with his parents in Parkston, he returned to Rapid City, this time with an engagement ring burning a hole in his pocket. Irene agreed to his proposal and a June wedding was planned. The second bit of good news for Kurtenbach was that he learned he had been accepted as a summer intern for General Electric in Syracuse, New York. His summer with GE was further rewarded because he was selected by the company to help test the firm's first prototype of a very large, ground-based long-range radar set. He believes his contacts with General Electric equipment and personnel in Korea and Texas probably helped in his selection.

But before helping design and build radar sets, there was a wedding to attend to. Because the Catholic Church in Irene's hometown had recently burned down, the ceremony was held in a little church in nearby Draper. Friends and relatives from the Dimock and Parkston area, and Irene's family and friends at the wedding, added up to considerably more people than the entire population of the small eastern Jones County community of 120. After the ceremony and a reception in the Murdo High School's gymnasium, and another reception 200 miles away in Parkston the following Monday, the new Kurtenbach family packed their few possessions into the 1950 Plymouth and headed for the summer job in Syracuse. The journey included a memorable side trip to Niagara Falls, after which Kurtenbach, with his characteristic easy smile, assured Irene that she was most probably the only Murdo, South Dakota, girl to have ever honeymooned at Niagara Falls.

The newlyweds rented a small cabin, actually a converted garage, on Lake Onida, and settled in for two months of work and weekend explorations of interesting sites. Kurtenbach considered the experience with General Electric that summer as valuable for his future career as a teacher and entrepreneur. "It provided me with valuable exposure to corporate life in a project environment," he recalled. The summer of 1960, he later learned, was the year that Jack Welch, who was destined to become chairman and Chief Executive Officer of General Electric, joined the firm. And it did not go unnoticed to Kurtenbach that Welch had earned his doctorate in chemistry by that time. This helped in Kurtenbach's thought process later when he considered the possibility of earning his doctorate degree.

But first, Kurtenbach concentrated on earning a bachelor's degree. With his internship at General Electric completed, Aelred and Irene steered their faithful Plymouth back to South Dakota in time for him to report to fall football camp. The

With his 1958 homecoming day beard, School of Mines student Aelred poses with his trademark supply of spare pens.

couple had been hired to live and work that fall on a small ranch just east of Rapid City in Rapid Valley owned by a Sioux Falls surgeon. In exchange for lodging, they helped with the chores and other duties of caring for a stable of competitive cutting horses. Irene also assisted with household activities and babysitting for the family. It was their first experience living in the country, and not surprisingly, they discovered that the lifestyle suited them perfectly. Today, they still prefer the quiet solitude of country living along the Big Sioux River south of Brookings.

The fall of 1960 was busy not only with the ranching responsibilities, but also with football. This, and Kurtenbach's tenure as president of the Student Body, ate away at his spare time for study. As a consequence, his grades were beginning to show it. More time to hit the books was made available after the rugged demands of football aggravated his long-suffering knee. Fortuitously, after surgery to repair torn cartilage just before Christmas, 1960, the recovery gave him long hours to spend with his nose in a book. His grades improved as he hobbled from class to class on into February of 1961 and his final semester (the state schools had finally switched to a semester system) of his bachelor's program. His senior year, he was selected as the Outstanding Electrical Engineering Student in recognition of his exceptional academic record and as a popular student leader.

That final semester of his senior year in 1961 also brought the thrilling news of an expected new arrival into the Kurtenbach family, and the important decision to apply for an assistantship as part of his quest to

June 11, 1960

65

earn a master's degree in electrical engineering. He and Irene decided that the offer from the University of Nebraska's Medical Electronics program best suited their future plans. The pay for the assistantship was $244 a month, and with judicious budgeting, they calculated they could survive on that.

The spring of 1961 was unique for Kurtenbach's parents, John and Theodora, who were working out the difficult but joyous logistics that would make it possible for them to attend the college graduation ceremonies of three of their children. DeWayne was to graduate from Southern State College in Springfield in eastern South Dakota, followed by Aelred's graduation a few days later on June 2 in western South Dakota at the School of Mines, and then a quick trip back to the extreme eastern side of the state, at Brookings, where Frank was set to graduate from South Dakota State University. They managed to attend every ceremony. Of John and Theodora's nine children, six went on to earn college degrees.

After the graduation ceremony, during which Kurtenbach was recognized as an Honor Student, he and Irene, with help from Kurtenbach's brothers Ivan and Wilfred and his wife, packed the trusted Plymouth, and a little red trailer that Kurtenbach had acquired, for the next stop in their lives at the University of Nebraska. Because the baby was to arrive about two weeks after graduation, their journey to Lincoln was delayed for a planned stop in Parkston to await Carla's arrival. She was born June 19, 1961, and as soon as she was able to travel, the now three-member Kurtenbach family headed to Lincoln where a small apartment would be their new home.

Carla, incidentally, went on to graduate from South Dakota State University in 1984 with a bachelor's degree in electrical engineering and minors in math and computer science. She worked as a college student at Daktronics, and after graduation because its full-time Systems Sales Engineer. Carla Gatzke earned a master's degree in business administration from Drake University and taught there for a semester in the Finance Department. Aelred and Irene's oldest child later returned to management positions at Daktronics and now serves as vice-president for Human Resources and is the corporate secretary.

For the rest of that summer after Carla's birth, however, Kurtenbach and three other graduate assistants commuted from Lincoln to nearby Omaha for classes at the University's College of Medicine, taking physiology, anatomy, and other life science courses. Kurtenbach said that he had always had an interest in medicine because some of the movements and functions of the human body could be replicated artificially with electricity, and this fascinated him. The artificial heart was an example, and before that mechanism was fully developed, he was privileged to witness open heart surgery at the hospital. At that time, such procedures were still in their pioneering days.

As the year of his study for a master's degree wound down, the Kurtenbachs were in search of a full-time employment. By that time Kurtenbach had decided that his short-term future would probably be working within a large corporation, so most of his scheduled interviews for work were in the northeast where many of the large corporations were headquartered.

He remembered distinctly what turned out to be a life-changing conversation during an interview with representatives of an electronics company in Long Island, New York. "At lunch that day one of the engineers asked from which airport I would be leaving," Kurtenbach remembered. It was John F. Kennedy International. "They told me to be sure to take a seat on the right hand side of the airplane because with the wind conditions, the plane would probably take off and bank left. They encouraged me to look out of the airplane window for the ribbon of red tail-lights of commuters driving home for the day. The ribbon would extend as far into the distance as the eye could see, they told me."

Kurtenbach is grateful today for that bit of aircraft seating advice. "As I looked out the plane's window, I saw what the engineer had described and I realized that I could not deal with that kind of congestion," he said. The revelation was as if an out-of-focus camera had suddenly snapped into sharp and clear focus for him. When he got home, he told Irene of that red-lined aerial panorama, and they both, the two small town South Dakotans who favored country life away from the hustle and bustle, agreed that they would seek their future somewhere in the Midwest, possibly South Dakota.

Kurtenbach suspected the engineers who advised him of the aerial view were probably aware of what a difficult adjustment to big city life it would be for the country boy that he was, and they wanted him to realize what would be in store for him if he left that rural environment. He is thankful for the visual lesson they brought to his attention.

About that time, another well-timed experience helped point him to a future in the university classroom. "I was asked to give a lecture in one of the classes I was taking. I wasn't looking forward to it, but as I got into that lecture I found out that it was not as bad as I had envisioned. I discovered that I might actually enjoy teaching," he said.

To his delight, he learned there were teaching positions in electrical engineering available in South Dakota for which he qualified. He accepted the offer from South Dakota State University's College of Engineering. With able assistance from Irene in the days before computer word processing software made typing a much less arduous task, Kurtenbach completed his master's thesis on time and graduated from the University of Nebraska in August of 1962.

As it was with the completion of his bachelor's degree and the graduation ceremony, "we had another of those totally chaotic, jam-packed graduation and moving days," Kurtenbach remembered. On graduation day, he completed his final examination early in the morning. Then, with the help of friends, the Kurtenbachs began packing all that they owned, which wasn't much, into the Plymouth and their trailer, completing the task by about 6 p.m., leaving enough time to prepare for the graduation ceremony at 7 p.m.

Kurtenbach considered it important that he attend the graduation, even though it was not required. A university policy levied a charge of $25 for those who missed the ceremony. The Kurtenbach family didn't have that kind of extra money, equivalent to a couple of gas tank refills to get them to Brookings. So with the graduation ceremony over and a final round of last-minute packing completed, the Kurtenbach Plymouth, again loaded with all that they owned, took them north to Brookings, South Dakota.

A night of driving was necessary because of their car's faulty cooling system that would have been further strained during the heat of the day. So, with the car stuffed to the gunnels and a sagging trailer weaving along behind them, the Kurtenbachs and blissful Carla filling the front seat, the trio made it to Brookings. They arrived early the next morning at his sister Eva and brother-in-law Everett's tiny student housing barracks on campus. Everett at the time was a student at South Dakota State University.

Later in the day of house hunting, they rented a first floor apartment in a house built by an SDSU icon, Dr. Halvor Solberg, distinguished professor of engineering. Solberg had designed what became Solberg Hall, which was assigned to the College of Engineering. Kurtenbach would one day teach classes in it. The home they lived in at that time was eventually torn down, and the site is now the location of the university's Pierson Residence Hall.

The $25 saved by attending graduation in Lincoln had long since been expended for gasoline on the trip north, so funds in the Kurtenbach coffers were limited. Until classes started that September, the month their second child was expected, Kurtenbach found a job working for The Spitznagel Partners (TSP) in Sioux Falls. Coincidentally, the firm needed help completing the electrical plans for Shepard Hall to be built on the South Dakota State University campus not far from the Kurtenbach's first floor apartment.

The job at TSP was expected to last about four weeks. Kurtenbach commuted daily to the firm's headquarters in Sioux Falls, sharing the driving with his brother-in-law, who was by then working with Best Business Machines.

On Sept. 18, 1962, the Kurtenbach's second daughter, Paula, was born at the Brookings Hospital, which is now West Hall, converted for university use after the city's new hospital was built.

Kurtenbach has fond memories of that first year at South Dakota State University, not only because of the arrival of his second daughter, but also because he discovered that he very much enjoyed teaching and research. He remembers many of his students from that first year, including Ron Schmidt, who enrolled in Kurtenbach's Circuits Synthesis class. Schmidt eventually became the owner of Zytec, a company that had manufacturing facilities at Redwood Falls, Minnesota, in the 1990s. In later years, whenever their paths crossed, Schmidt took great pleasure in joshing his former college mentor about the infamous first test Kurtenbach gave to the class. No one received a grade higher than a "C."

"I didn't intend to, but I guess I did make it a little too difficult. We still have a fun talking about that test," Kurtenbach said.

When not teaching, Kurtenbach enjoyed being a part of a research team headed by Dr. Arthur Dracy of the university's Dairy Science Department. The somewhat unusual research effort sought to determine the extent and the intricacies of bloating in dairy cattle, a very real problem having signifi-

As a boy Aelred had the pony Prince. Daughters Carla and Paula had dad.

cant financial impact. The unsuspecting star of the research was a cow named Campanile Double Raven Ina. She probably wasn't happy about her new role in life, especially after Kurtenbach and Dracy rigged her up for field recordings of stomach pressure readings that were then broadcast from Ina's pasture back to a central station that Kurtenbach developed. Kurtenbach applied some of the medical electronics experiences he had received at the University of Nebraska, and this proved valuable to the research.

The Kurtenbachs were eventually able to purchase their first home, a 1,000-square foot house with an unfinished basement located at 208 17th Avenue. The first-time homeowners were ecstatic. "Frankly, we both thought we'd died and gone to heaven after so many years of living in tiny, cramped apartments," Kurtenbach remembers.

That summer of 1963 also brought more good news. Kurtenbach was accepted to take part in a Ford Foundation program at Penn State University that addressed engineering education. It was intended for new engineering instructors, helping them develop procedures to be more effective in the

Reece Kurtenbach is baptisted at St. Thomas More church in Brookings by Fr. Tony Emberi. Sisters Carla, right, and Paula, were there.

classroom. After that first Circuits Synthesis test that Ron Schmidt and his classmates remembered so well, Kurtenbach welcomed the opportunity to improve his teaching techniques.

On August 11, 1964, son Reece, named after Kurtenbach's School of Mines friend, was born. Like his older sister, he, too, would grow up to become an important leader at Daktronics. August was also the month that Congress passed the Gulf of Tonkin Resolution, which approved US military intervention in Southeast Asia that led to full-scale war in Vietnam.

During the school year that fall, Kurtenbach and his wife decided it was time for him to move forward in his profession. He would seek a doctorate degree. "I had been teaching for three years and decided that if I was going to be in education, I needed to get a doctoral degree, so I conned Irene into letting me do that," he laughed. It was a difficult decision for him. It would surely mean more sacrifices for Irene and the children. But after discussing it, Irene not only agreed but was encouraging and supportive. So with a leave of absence from South Dakota State University and a much-needed $10,000 loan from the Ford Foundation that was established to assist young engineers in pursing the Ph.D. degree, Kurtenbach prepared for study at Purdue University.

"We started planning for another transition, and here we go again," he recalled. That migration to Purdue first meant a trip in the other direction for a National Science Foundation ten-week course on Linear Algebra at the University of Colorado. Before leaving for Colorado, there was the sad task of selling their beloved first home and finding a place in Brookings to store their furniture and other belongings not needed in Colorado. The transition also included trading off their faithful old Plymouth that had served them both so well for so many years. They moved up in the automotive field but still couldn't afford a new car. Instead, they acquired a used 1961 Ford Falcon station wagon. This would serve them well until the summer of 1970 when the family began a major transition of starting a new company called Daktronics.

They located a small, one bedroom apartment just across the street from the University of Colorado campus. With no television and on a limited budget, Kurtenbach and Irene read mystery novels for entertainment, and the family dined often on macaroni and cheese. They also enjoyed brief jaunts in the Rocky Mountains between Denver and Ft. Collins. Friends from Brookings, Bob and Margaret Heil, lived in Ft. Collins, and the Kurtenbach family also visited Bud Laber, who was at the time engaged to Kurtenbach's sister Alice, (they were married that November). Time was also spent with the Jim Mergenhausers, old friends from high school in Parkston. Jim was working on his doctorate in chemistry at the university.

After ten weeks in Colorado it was time to head for studies in Purdue. Kurtenbach and Irene, by now expert automobile packers, loaded the kids and their meager belongings in their car and first drove back to South Dakota to pick up a few more of their personal items. With a trailer loaded and the car packed with kids and other belongings, they headed to West Lafayette just before Labor Day in 1965.

The trip included an overnight stop at Keokuk, Iowa, where Kurtenbach's brother Frank was then teaching and coaching in the Keokuk High School. The Kurtenbachs arrived about 10 p.m., and with a house full of frolicksome, wide awake children, one-year-old Reece, in the excitement of the moment, managed to fall off a rocking horse, resulting in a late-night trip to the Keokuk hospital emergency room for stitches to the top of his head. The thin lining of an egg, a traditional Kurtenbach treatment for cuts, was apparently not included in the Keokuk Hospital protocol.

At Purdue, the Kurtenbachs moved into a two bedroom apartment in one of the school's married student housing units. Close and good neighbors included Bill and Margaret Mow. Bill would later start several companies, including Bugle Boy, a popular clothing company. They were also good friends with Jerry and Delphine Cardello, who now live in California, and Friend Bechtel and his wife LuAnn.

Kurtenbach registered for the fall semester in Purdue's Electrical Engineering College's Communications and Information Theory program, partly because of its outstanding faculty. He quickly waded into the demanding academic regimen required. He selected Professor John Hancock as his faculty advisor and that first semester he also taught an Electrical Engineering Problems Laboratory. Among his students was Hugh Jager, who later switched from engineering to earn a law degree. Kurtenbach didn't recall the name from his first class, but when Jager eventually became Daktronics' patent attorney, he reminded his former engineering teacher of the coincidence.

Kurtenbach also had to contend with passing the school's qualifying examination scheduled for late November of 1965. With that important hurdle successfully cleared, he set his course on completion of that first semester of work. By now he had a new advisor, Dr. Paul Wintz, after Dr. Hancock had been promoted to head of the department. Kurtenbach and Wintz were about the same age, and between the two of them, a number of top-level writings were published in the various divisions of the IEEE transactions, which are the most significant publications for Electrical Engineering faculty.

During his final year of doctorate preparation, the summer of 1966, Kurtenbach decided to take additional classes to become more proficient in higher mathematics. Another student, Keith Stromsmo, had the same idea, and the Kurtenbachs became good friends with Keith and Betty Ann. Keith is now retired from the faculty of the University of Alberta in Edmonton, Canada. The Stromsmo-Kurtenbach partnership in higher mathematics was interrupted about midway through the summer when the Kurtenbachs learned that they were expecting their fourth child. It was on one of Irene's regular visits to the doctor during that time that she was advised to stop smoking. Kurtenbach decided to join in the effort, and together they succeeded, and remain forever grateful for their decision.

Kurtenbach's doctoral dissertation was a computer simulation of a digital communications system accomplished with the aid of a research grant that paid for a quarter time assistantship plus computer time and clerical work. "I analyzed the quality of the system under the influence of the three noise sources that are inherent in a digital communications system," he explained. The noises, he said, are the sampling noise, the quantizing noise, and the channel noise. Kurtenbach tested the varying levels of the three noise sources using a mean square error measurement as the metric, he said.

While his Ph.D dissertation was on the study of noise sources, it included lessons for a future businessman, too, That was because of the aspects of random sampling in his research. "Engineering is a rather broad training base," Kurtenbach said. "Studying an engineering system prepares you to study any system. The thought process is the same and the world of uncertainty is very important in the business world."

With that dissertation completed and his oral examination over, the family prepared to return to Brookings and South Dakota State University shortly before Christmas of 1967. Graduating from Purdue wouldn't officially occur until the following June, so with help from friends, former South Dakotans Duane and Teresa Fowler, the car and the trailer were packed, sandwiches were made, and the Falcon wagon headed west. That automobile trip would probably be the most memorable of all for the traveling Kurtenbach family. Lisa, the newest member, had been born February 16, 1967, and earned a front seat position with her parents on the long ride back to South Dakota.

The car's heater functioned passably, but in the sub-zero weather on that trip back, it was obvious that the weather would win the contest. No one in the car would be exceptionally comfortable. With the station wagon packed with four kids and some of the family's personal items, the growing Kutenbach clan left at about 6 p.m. and headed for South Dakota. As planned, they stopped at a Holiday Inn at LaSalle, Illinois, later that night. On the road again early the next morning, the weather deteriorated. By the time they crossed the Mississippi River, an ice storm forced them to seek a port to wait out the storm. They found refuge in an Iowa City motel. By mid-afternoon, conditions seemed to have improved, so the family headed west again on busy Interstate 80, where the semi trucks travel in packs headed for Omaha and points west. The unplanned and unbudgeted stop in Iowa City had consumed their hotel money set aside for the trip. So they decided to drive straight through to Brookings, which meant a full night of Interstate travel.

The weather turned bitter cold as they headed north toward South Dakota. The kids were dressed warmly and zippered into the family's double-sized sleeping bags laid out in the back of the station wagon. Lisa, the baby, was up front nearer the cranky heater, and also wearing her heavy snow suit. It was the parents who noticed the temperature change. The heater was deficient and their feet were feeling numb. For them, it was a miserable trip home. They could hardly wait to get to the new house at 1312 Fifth Street in Brookings they had recently purchased. They finally pulled into town about 3 a.m. on Dec. 22, 1967. The temperature was a toe-numbing thirty degrees below zero. While they were carrying sleepy kids and a few of their belongings into the house, alert and curious Brookings police pulled up to investigate what this vagabond family in the old station wagon with a U-Haul trailer tagging on behind was doing entering an empty house in the dark of night.

The next day, Kurtenbach hurried out hoping to find a Christmas tree for the kids. He found a scrawny, leftover tree, and with just a few gifts under it for each member of the family, Christmas 1967 passed by happily.

Over the first week of the New Year, 1968, Kurtenbach drove back to Indiana to complete the necessary filings of his dissertation with the library and the graduate office, and to do what was necessary to prepare for graduation in June. He also packed up the U-Haul trailer with the family's remaining furniture, and drove back to Brookings. The spring semester started at South Dakota State University in late January.

During that spring semester of 1968, he had become acquainted with another South Dakotan, Duane Sander, a former Howard High School Tiger football team end who, like Kurtenbach, was raised on a farm, this one near Howard, South Dakota. Sander was also a graduate of South Dakota School of Mines and Technology (1960) with masters and doctoral degrees from Iowa State. Dr. Sander was also teaching in the South Dakota State University Electrical Engineering Department. Kurtenbach and Sander, both country boys with degrees from the School of Mines, shared common experiences and became close friends. They began to talk about working together to start a company of some sort. They didn't have any idea what sort of company they would form or how it would be financed, but they were determined to settle in on a niche in the then "go-go" times for electronics. Those conversations that took place in between their duties teaching classes and laboratories were the first discussions on what would, before year's end, become Daktronics, Inc.

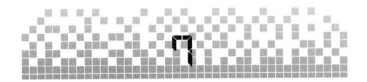

The "Wow" Factor

About seven thousand cubic feet of concrete was in place and setting quickly in the dry Texas heat. The enormous footings, six of them, were designed to support a massive 290-ton steel superstructure held upright and in place with anchor bolts sporting heads five inches in diameter.

With all in place in the late summer of 2006, it was now up to Daktronics Senior Project Manager Jody Kress, 34, and his crew to install the remaining 52 tons of wires, harnesses, LED panels, computers, and a plethora of other electronic gizmos hitched in sequence and working in concert to bring life and excitement to the world's largest ever scoreboard and video display. All this performing power would eat up 2,000 amps. An average home uses about 200, so a platoon of forty whirring five-ton air conditioners were tasked to prevent a meltdown in the Texas heat.

Adding to the challenge of building the world's largest sports scoreboard was the time frame start to finish. There wasn't much time for all of this to happen, but Kress and his support staff back at Daktronics in Brookings knew that when they accepted the job for the University of Texas' Royal-Memorial Stadium in Austin.

The contract was signed on May 8, 2006, for what would be the mother of all scoreboards to be completed in four months before the Texas Longhorns opening game that fall. Daktronics engineers had designed, built, and installed thousands of scoreboards all over the world, so they had the time required for the installation phase almost down to the hour and minute. But there were other factors involved, including the weather, and with each step in the evolution of their unique displays over the preceding years, everything became more complicated, and there was always the possibility of something going wrong somewhere in the maze of wires and light emitting diodes and all the rest. Usually, a project of this approximate size and scope took about twelve months from the design-build phase at the Brookings plant to installation and final testing at the site. The decision to accept the job with such an almost impossible short time-line came about after a typical "we'll all work together" meeting of the engineers, assemblers and technicians at Daktronics. Kress was given the responsibility to coordinate it all from start to finish.

When up and humming as planned, the big board would be over twenty times the size of the makeshift basketball court the young Kurtenbach boys set up in the dusty hayloft of their dad's barn back on the farm near Dimock, South Dakota. That was back when the term solid state was probably a politician's term for a state operating in the black and when the word LED was a gold mining town in the Black Hills.

Stretching 134 feet long and 55 feet high, as wide as a football field, the Texas scoreboard and high definition video display would deliver game information and crisp instant replays and advertising messages, interspersed with flashing animation created by Daktronics' talented computer graphic artists who guaranteed their work would whip up the crowd at the reigning national champion Longhorns' opening game of the season against North Texas State.

Kress had made periodic trips to Austin during the early spring to seal the $8 million sale and to line up contractors for the preliminary concrete and steel work. It was critical that the concrete was placed and poured into footing holes 32 feet deep, as Daktronics site engineers had specified, albeit in more scientific terms. The University of Texas was busy upgrading its utility capacity to meet the demands of the big board.

Meanwhile, back at the Daktronics plant in Brookings, as a huge crane set the steel infrastructure in place in Austin, technicians were preparing the board and screen's hardware and software needs. The video screen, with Daktronics' own ProStar® technology, was huge. Think of it as a television set about the size of your home. ProStar® provided crisp, clear, color-true renditions right down to the laces of the football. It had the highest resolution of any screen of that size ever built.

The panels, 36 in all, with their five million light emitting diodes and the other electronic marvels necessary for the scoreboard, were loaded on semi-trucks at the Brookings plant. Over a period of several days they left Brookings for the long drive to Austin. In all, over a dozen big trucks made the trip, carrying the parts in sequence as they would be needed at the site.

Kress, a native of Monticello, MN, and an Electrical Engineering Tech-

The gigantic Daktronics scoreboard and video display at the University of Texas, Austin.

nology graduate of South Dakota State University, caught a flight down to begin the task of installation and testing before the big football game that was now weeks away.

Once everything had been properly placed in the supporting superstructure, the top of the big board where Kress and the others would often work was as high as a six-story building. Kress and a small contingent from the Brookings plant would spend twelve to fifteen hour days scrambling up and down the maze of catwalks. They meticulously tested every aspect of the scoreboard and computerized video display as concerned University of Texas athletic officials counted the days and hours before opening game day of the football season.

Down below on the field, members of the Longhorn football team went through their paces, all the while keeping a curious eye on the big board's progress. They were impressed. "Oh man, that thing's big," commented wide receiver Quan Cosby. "At night, we don't need the lights it's so bright." It wasn't long before team members, and everyone else in Austin and in Texas were calling the big board "Godzillatron," coined by a Longhorn fan watching the progress on an Internet site.

Everything snapped into place and the testing proved out with no time to spare. With just two hours before the opening kick-off, all was ready. Kress, a former linebacker for his high school football team and a huge South Dakota State University Jackrabbit football fan, remembers that he didn't watch much of the Longhorn versus North Texas State game. With a record 85,124 fans in the stadium, he didn't want the big Daktronics display to fall on its face. It didn't. Godzillatron won over the fans and exceeded all expectations. All of its millisecond bells and whistles functioned as intended. It was a happy day for Longhorn fans. A new scoreboard that mirrored the excellence, the future, and the forward thinking of the University of Texas had debuted, and the final score was frosting on the cake: University of Texas, 56, North Texas, 7. Daktronics had scored again, too, as it had so many times before and would continue to do with its famous "wow" factor displays.

A few months before the 2006 National Football League season, other Daktronics engineers supervised the placement of North America's largest high definition, LED video boards in Dolphin Stadium in Miami. The boards helped entertain the 74,000 fans attending the 2007 Super Bowl, including CBS-TV's Andy Rooney. Two giant high definition video replay screens are located at each end of the stadium. Imagine resolution was impressive. Rooney, commenting on attending the Super Bowl during his popular *60 Minutes* segment on Feb. 11, 2007, said that watching the two video display screens in Dolphin Stadium was like sitting at home watching the game on television.

M. Bruce Schulze, president of Dolphin Stadium, was also impressed. "The two high definition video displays from Daktronics, along with the Daktronics fascia display, played key roles in providing our guests with an amazing Super Bowl experience," he said. "We are extremely happy with the Daktronics system," Those two displays and the fascia display Schulze mentioned are loaded with more than nine million individual red, green and blue light emitting diodes (LEDs), and they make the high definition imagery possible.

Daktronics systems have had important roles in past Super Bowl games as well. Detroit's Ford Field, host of the 2006 Super Bowl, and Alltel Stadium in Jacksonville, host of the 2005 Super Bowl, both counted on Dak-

A video panel is hoisted in to place at Dolphin Stadium.

Frame work of one of the huge Daktronics dispays at Dolphin Stadium, Miami, that is ready for installation of the video panels with their remarkable resolution.

The east end zone Daktronics video display, Dolphin Stadium, Miami, FL.

tronics super systems for fan enhancement and entertainment. NFL venues in Glendale, AZ, and Tampa, FL, will host 2008 and 2009 Super Bowl games and both stadiums already use Daktronics super systems. The 2010 Super Bowl returned to Miami's Dolphin Stadium.

Ironically, designing, manufacturing, marketing, and servicing big sporting scoreboard displays like the one at the University of Texas and at Dolphin Stadium wasn't exactly what Kutenbach and Daktronics co-founder Duane Sander had in mind when they and their wives were mulling over business opportunities in 1968. While a specific niche hadn't been targeted, both men knew that transistor logic had almost unlimited possibilities.

They at first were thinking much smaller, planning to provide electronic biomedical instrumentation. Kurtenbach had always had a fascination with medicine, and graduate work at the University of Nebraska had further piqued his interest. So the digital thermometer and something called a sphygmomanometer, the instruments they were hoping to market, have, over the years of Daktronic's phenomenal growth, evolved into the amazing, gigantic, glitzy Godzillatron-like displays and hundreds of other applications worldwide.

The vision of Daktronics into something far different than biomedical

One part of the Daktronics presence at Raymond James Stadium, home of the Tampa Bay Buccaneers and site of the NFL Super Bowl XXXV.

applications came about while Aelred Kurtenbach was reading the *Wall Street Journal* one afternoon. The State of Utah was looking for a company to make and install an electronic voting system in its House of Representatives. But that came after the long and difficult process of just getting Daktronics started.

The idea for starting a business of some kind took root in Kurtenbach's mind when he was working on his doctorate at Purdue. "While I was there I took an undergraduate course in personal finance which touched on investing and evaluating corporate financial statements," Kurtenbach said. The mid-1960s were often referred to in the world of electronics as the "go-go" years. At the time, the term "high tech" wasn't in common usage. High tech or not, new electronics companies were popping up all over the country. The opportunities in the emerging field of electronics were often discussed by Kurtenbach and other Purdue students. Some of his friends eventually did start companies, and the thought occurred to Kurtenbach that perhaps he could, too. The course in financing was the first business course in which he had ever enrolled during all of his educational endeavors, and it helped nudge him farther into the possibility of starting a business.

Kurtenbach's forte until then had always been more on the technical and scientific side, beginning with those old automobile magneto magnets that amazed him and started his fertile mind to spinning at the Sts. Peter and Paul Grade School in Dimock, and the dashboard electronics of the old Plymouth he and his brothers drove until it dropped. So he was surprised that the course in financing so interested him. "I found that I enjoyed the class tremendously, and I learned that financial analysis was not that difficult. The course piqued my interest in financing and investing, and it complemented the other discussions we were all having during those 'go-go' years about electronics start-up companies."

"A number of graduate students from electrical engineering took the class, and there was a lot of discussion about entrepreneurship among the students at Purdue," he said. Kurtenbach didn't fully realize it at the time, but what would become Daktronics was simmering somewhere in his subconscious psyche. "Exciting things were happening then in the world of electronics—a lot of change was taking place—and I was looking for my niche in all of that," he said.

Today he traces the roots of his flair for entrepreneurship to growing up on the Dimock farm and to intellectual contacts at Purdue while taking the course in finance, as well as being at the cutting edge of the integrated circuits era that was beginning to transform the world of electronics.

The business of farming, which he often talked about with his father, also helped set his eventual course. "We talked about farming and we talked about strategies to use and what equipment might need to be bought and what needed to be repaired," he said. "We talked about what livestock we should retain for breeding purposes to build the herd and what livestock should be sold for income to support the family, so we got involved in a lot of those discussions that are just basic to running a business. It really doesn't matter so much how many zeros are behind the numbers. The rationale and reasoning for the decisions turns out to be the same for farming or for any other business."

After Purdue, when the Kurtenbach family returned to Brookings, he met another electrical engineer and faculty member, Dr. Duane Sander. "We became close friends and we eventually decided to start a company."

That came after many long, serious discussions between classes, in the evenings, and on weekends at backyard barbecues or Sunday dinners with Phyllis Sander and Irene joining in. "One of our intentions at that time was to offer an alternative to university graduates who were leaving the state and area for opportunities elsewhere," Kurtenbach said. Both professors knew many young people in their classes who wanted to find jobs in a familiar environment without having to go to a big city. Kurtenbach knew the feeling. That long red line of vehicle tail lights he saw from his airplane seat returning from an East Coast interview years before was still etched in his mind.

"Duane and I thought there was potential in South Dakota, and it seemed while everyone talked about it, no one was doing anything to try to keep young people here," he said. The two professors viewed young men and women at the university not only as personable, bright, and talented young citizens, but as potential assets for a company. "And that was one part of our initial hypothesis that's turned out to be true," Kurtenbach said. "We see a high degree of quality in the graduates of South Dakota State University. And because we are located so close to the college physically and psychologically, we now have many students working part-time with us at any given time. It's like an extended interview. And that's a real advantage," Kurtenbach continued, "because we have a long time to look them over under actual production conditions."

The Daktronics co-founder considers the firm's location in the nation's midsection, in a relatively poor state that is rich in talented young people, as one of the company's competitive edges. "In fact, I would say that our major strength is location," Kurtenbach said. "We have a strong educational base here. We're able to get the top people in South Dakota and they're as good as the top people anywhere. We can hire people at a better rate because they have a better life here. There are few hassles."

There is a noticeable esprit de corps among the Daktonics family that now numbers in excess of 3,000 worldwide. Employee after employee talks about their pride in the company and in its products, particularly the ones they helped to design, build or install. They take it all personally. And they are willing to go the extra mile or work the extra hour to insure product quality and customer satisfaction.

"Our business climate here is consistently rated among the best in the nation. We have a wonderful, supportive state and a beautiful town to live in. And we have a steady supply of talented and motivated people, so in my opinion we have the best of all worlds right here in the heart of America," Kurtenbach said.

Kurtenbach, Sander, and fellow electrical engineering professor Dr. Virgil Ellerbruch spent the summer of 1968 writing chapters for a book on integrated circuits that Electrical Engineering Department Head Dr. Frank Fitchen was putting together. At the same time, Sander and Kurtenbach, neophytes in the world of business, continued to dream and talk about the possibility of starting a business. By the late summer of 1968 they had decided to call a meeting of people in the Brookings area with differing backgrounds and professional training and expertise, to discuss possible avenues a business might take. About thirty people attended a meeting in a basement classroom of Crothers Engineering Hall on the university campus. Many possibilities were discussed during that exploratory session.

After the meeting ended and everyone else had left, Kurtenbach and Sander slouched in front row chairs in the empty room and reviewed what had been said. "Finally, we looked at one another and almost simultaneously came to the conclusion that if we were going to get a company started, we needed to do it ourselves," Kurtenbach recalls. "So that's the moment when we decided to start a company and to call it Daktronics, a name I had earlier talked to Duane about."

They later conferred with a young Brookings attorney, Lewayne Erickson, who was a friend of Sander from Howard, South Dakota. Erickson met with the two couples one evening at the Sander home. They discussed the legal requirements of starting a new company and the difficulties and the pitfalls involved. It was decided that Erickson would draft the necessary papers.

Articles of Incorporation forming Daktronics, Inc., were signed by Duane and Phyllis Sander and Aelred and Irene Kurtenbach on Dec. 9, 1968. Kurtenbach would be the president, and Phyllis Sander vice-president. Her husband Duane was named the secretary-treasurer and Irene became the assistant secretary. Remembers Phyllis of the signing of the papers: "We were all optimistic and maybe a bit apprehensive of what was to happen to our new Daktronics, Inc." Not everyone in Brookings shared the same enthusiasm. Naysayers comfortable in their world were rolling eyes and shaking heads. Early encouragement of the launching, however, was not lacking in the minds of the university President, Dr. H. M. Briggs, nor with Dr. Frank Fitchen, head of the university's Electrical Engineering Department. "Early on we met with them and outlined our plans since they were our employers and we needed to know if what we were about to do would reflect upon our employment," Kurtenbach said. "Both men were sympathetic, encouraging, and reassuring about what we were about to do."

Each co-founder put $1,000 into a new Daktronics checking account in the First National Bank in Brookings, now First Bank & Trust. "Our families at that time were young and expanding, and we had no cash, but we did find $1,000 to spare," Kurtenbach said. "We were rich in children and poor in dollars," he added.

They soon realized that they would need more investors to reach the threshold goal of about $50,000, so Kurtenbach and Sander researched their options. They decided that they could raise money through a small public offering, since discontinued, known as a Regulation A that Congress had authorized for exactly what Kurtenbach and Sander were trying to do. They were able under this legislation to raise money by selling stock that was not being traded on the Exchange.

A 16-page typed prospectus was prepared and approved by the Denver Office of the Securities Exchange Commission. Under Regulation A, Kurtenbach and Sander as corporation principals could sell stock themselves rather than working through an investment banking firm. "We realized we were not going to get a company started in a short period of time, so in our prospectus we made provisions of raising additional money in the three-year period following the Initial Public Offering," Kurtenbach said.

Units, or shares, would sell for $5. Slightly fewer than 50,000 shares were made available with the hopes of raising $250,000. Included in the articles was an introduction that included a 145-word sentence listing why the company had been organized and what it intended to do… "to invent, develop, produce, construct, fabricate, acquire, market, manufacture, lease, sell…etc." The articles included a contemplated use for the income from the stock sales for the firm's first year of operation. This included $2,000 for purchase and rental of equipment, $2,400 for supplies, and most of the rest for wages for "a full-time engineer, two part-time engineers, secretarial help, one full-time technician and one part-time technician." The $47,010 was

considered the minimum necessary to begin work as a corporation, and that dollar
figure was the threshold needed before the
concept Kurtenbach and Sander shared
could be kicked into overdrive.

At the time, Sander was working on
an electronic thermometer for hospital
and medical uses and Kurtenbach was
devising an automatic sphygmomanometer, a six-syllable word for a means to
measure blood pressure. Coincidentally—
and fortuitously—a graduate student,
James Morgan, was using Kurtenbach's
sphygmomanometer research as the sub-
ject of his master's degree project. Morgan
would become one of the new firm's first
employees, and thirty years later become
Daktronics' chief executive officer.

A prototype Daktronics thermometer that was never marketed.

With the Securities Exchange Commission's blessings of their Regulation A
plan, Kurtenbach and Sander made the rounds visiting with friends, relatives, and associates in the Brookings area and the state, selling units of
stock and warrants at $5 per unit. "We had individual meetings, small
group meetings, we'd talk to friends we met on the street, whatever we
could do to tell our story," Kurtenbach said. All this wasn't easy for Kurtenbach. An intensely private man, he had to break from his shell and become
an aggressive salesman. The fact that he believed in what he was selling
made it easier for him, and his approach to friends, relatives, and colleagues
was always low key.

Two of the early investors in the company were Kurtenbach's teachers
in Parkston. Mrs. June (Arlo) Jones remembers the day Kurtenbach came to
Parkston to ask for financial help for the new company. "One of the things
my late husband Arlo and I admired about Aelred was his dedication to the
challenge of starting Daktronics," said the teacher who had taught typing to
Kurtenbach. Her husband, Arlo, had been Kurtenbach's high school history
teacher and was also his Future Farmers of America basketball team coach.

"Aelred approached Arlo one day and asked him to invest $1,000 in stock," Mrs. Jones said. "Arlo told him we couldn't afford that much at that time, so Aelred said he would give us three years to pay for it." Mrs. Jones said that's what she and her husband elected to do. "We accepted and through the years Daktronics has been good to us," she said.

So thanks to the Jones and many others, that first stock offering resulted in sale of 9,402 units to sixty-three South Dakotans. With that threshold goal sufficient for a year's operating capitol assured, Daktronics was off the dime and ready to begin serious operations. Easier said than done, as the co-founders were to learn.

A nine-inch news story, the first press release from the new company, was written by Craig Lawrence, a young editor-reporter for the *Brookings Register*. It announced that the new firm would "deal in electronic sub-contracting, specialty design, service and maintenance of laboratory equipment, and will develop and manufacture a line of electronic equipment for hospital, clinic and laboratory use."

Lawrence left the *Brookings Register* after two years and later launched the very successful advertising firm of Lawrence and Schiller in Sioux Falls. Years later, he reminisced about his first meeting with Kurtenbach for the 1968 story interview, and subsequent meetings when he helped Daktonics as a consultant. "In all my years of doing what I do now, and before that as a newspaper editor and reporter, I have never met anyone like him," he said. Kurtenbach had an "almost child-like imagination and a mirth-filled optimism." Lawrence remembered accompanying Kurtenbach on business trips to create interest in a Daktronics product.

Lawrence and the Kurtenbachs, Frank and Aelred, attended a meeting with the R. J. Reynolds Tobacco Company in Winston-Salem, NC. "The morning before the meeting with Reynolds officials, Al and I stopped at a restaurant for breakfast. When the waitress came to seat us, Al asked for a 'non-smoking' area. Now in the tobacco capitol of the world, Winston-Salem, that is a major fax paux," Lawrence said. The surprised waitress politely told Kurtenbach that in Winston-Salem, there are no non-smoking areas. Lawrence remembered that at the later meeting and during the Daktronics presentation, everyone in the R. J. Reynolds group lit up. "It wasn't long before the smoke was so thick that the light from our projector lamp could hardly get through to the screen," he laughed.

Lawrence listed three attributes that he believes sets Kurtenbach apart. He has an "unbridled imagination," he said, and his ability to harness the enthusiasm and energy of university students working for Daktronics impressed Lawrence. Kurtenbach, the quiet, almost bashful kid from Dimock, has a certain rapport that generates a synergisim to inspire Daktronics employees to dare to tackle difficult tasks. Finally, Lawrence is impressed with Kurtenbach's district sales organization strategy formed in the early days of the company. "I mean by that his decision to keep everyone near the home office, exposed to all aspects of the company, and then giving them responsibility by sending them out for sales, installation and service," he said. That renowned Daktronics teamwork and the ability for everyone, from the boss to the engineers to the technicians and custodians from different departments, to come together as a team is largely the work of Al Kurtenbach, Lawrence concluded.

Kutenbach often gave new employees some advice they did not expect to hear from him. He told them to go to college, but he backed that up with Daktronics scholarships, tuition waiver plans, special shifts between classroom schedules, and other incentives.

An example of Kurtenbach's rapport with young workers is well remembered by Joel DeBoer, who was hired in late 1976. Part of the interview process included a visit with Kurtenbach. "I was fresh off the farm," DeBoer remembered. "Here I was in the office of the company president for an interview." DeBoer said he was very nervous, but former farm boy Kurtenbach broke the ice. "We started talking about farming. I couldn't believe it. Here I am in the president's office for a job interview and we're talking about farming," DeBoer said.

Cheryl Dobesh, who started at Daktronics in 1976, remembers the time she was having difficulties in her personal life. "Al Kurtenbach happened to ask how I was doing and I mentioned them to him," she said. "That weekend he came to my house with an idea he thought might help."

One of Pam Schmidt's fondest Daktronics memories is from the early days when Kurtenbach walked around and handed out paychecks on payday. "He always shook everyone's hand and thanked them personally for working so hard for the company."

The very first Daktronics production line and front office were located in the western half of the tiny brick building just off Brookings' Main Avenue at 317 3rd St. The other half of the building was occupied by building owner Orville Duff, who operated Duff's Tire Shop. The space assigned to Daktronics was about twenty-feet by twenty-feet. Of course, Daktronics then was thinking small instrumentation, and its work force could fit in a Volkswagon, so space then was not a major concern.

Kurtenbach and Sander soon called their first meeting of the Daktronics stockholders in the basement community room of the First National Bank. At that first, historic stockholders session on June 30, 1969, a board of directors was elected. Seven Brookings residents who had purchased some of the 9,402 initial shares comprised the membership of that first board of directors.

Serving with the co-founders on the board were Robert Fishback of the First National Bank (now First Bank & Trust); Calvin Vaudrey, president of J. T. Banner and Associates, a local engineering consulting and design firm; Dr. John Sandfort, head of the Mechanical Engineering Department at South Dakota State University; Dr. Charles Roberts, a well-known and highly respected local physician; and Dr. John Uglum, an optometrist with the Watson Clinic of Brookings.

"They were a Godsend for us," Kurtenbach said. "Neither Duane or I had ever been in business before and we knew very little about running a business, but we were willing to burn the midnight oil and that's exactly what it took."

In their spare time over the next four years Kurtenbach and Sander continued to attempt to persuade others to invest in the remaining $200,000 in stock offerings while also teaching and managing the company. While many of their contacts did decide to invest, many did not want to get involved. "Some thought it was an impossible task and others thought we were just sort of crazy," Kurtenbach recalled. "I don't really think anyone bought shares because they saw it as a way to get wealthy, and I'm not sure many saw it as an investment opportunity either." But many considered it a way of doing something to help Brookings grow, he said.

In those early days, Kurtenbach and Sander were like the carnival plate spinners, rushing from one wobbly plate to another trying to keep all spinning and balanced atop spindly supports.

At the same time as the first stock offering, resulting in $47,010 cash in the Daktronics banking account to bring the firm to life, the Kurtenbach's fifth child, Matt, was born on June 26, 1969. He and the four other Kurtenbach children, three girls and two boys, would all grow up as Daktronics kids. All five Kurtenbach children earned degrees at South Dakota State University. Some of Matt's childhood memories are Daktronics-related, such as the popular company picnics at the Kurtenbach farm where cow milking contests were one of the hilarious games. "I also remember helping the family make hamburger patties for the picnics," Matt recalled. "All of us would gather around the kitchen table the night before, and even though the company was much smaller then, it still took a lot of hamburgers to feed everyone."

Matt, now an officer in the firm, also remembers as a young boy the many summer family vacations—not to visit monuments or scenic places—but to tour venues where Daktronics equipment was in operation or venues in which the firm hoped to install a system.

Neither Kurtenbach nor Sander, and none of the signers of the Articles of Incorporation or the early investors, knew then that within a few decades, the company they were helping to launch would become one of the world's leading suppliers of electronic scoreboards, large electronic display systems, marketing services, digital messaging solutions, and related software and services for sports, commercial, and transportation applications.

Becoming all of that would not happen quickly or easily. The University of Texas "Godzillatron" was still far in the future. And Daktronics' senior project director Jody Kress, who would be the company's site supervisor for the birth of the world's largest scoreboard, was himself yet to be born.

It was   propitious moment when—on a Friday evening in May of 1970—Kurtenbach spotted the *Wall Street Journal* article about the plans by the Utah House of Representative. The vision of Daktronics would soon change.

The fledgling firm's first big opportunity came with their successful bid for the design, fabrication, and installation of the new Salt Lake City system. The voting system market would tide Daktronics over and help nudge it through difficult growing pains. And it would give novices Kurtenbach and Sander confidence in their new company's ability to compete with the more established firms around the nation and the world.

But a friendship with a genial collegiate wrestling coach made years earlier would top even that *Wall Street Journal* tip.

Two huge Daktronics displays above busy Times Square in New York City. The Cola Cola creation below the Daktronics Samsung display is one of the most sophisticated and difficult ever designed, engineered and fabricated by Daktronics.

One of the unique Daktroncis displays created especially for the 1988 PGA Tour®. Power for the display, one of many on the course, is provided by the golf cart parked below the board, which is using the Glow Cube® technology.

There's a Daktronics touch is in the Charlotte Bobcat Arena where the largest video display screen of any National Basketball Association or National Hockey Association venue provide a resounding "wow" factor for Bobcat fans. Note the two narrow ProAd® facia displays in the bottom portion of the photograph.

Here's the famous and historic zipper sign in New York's Times Square. It was twice upgraded by Daktronics and now dances smartly around the building using the latest in LED technology.

The Oklahoma scoreboard display installed in 1997 was one of the first big screen displays for which Daktronics has become world-famous.

The outfield Daktronics display at Busch Stadium, home of the St. Louis Cardinals, is one of the most sophisticated placed in any major league ball field, providing photographs and statistics constantly up-dated during the game.

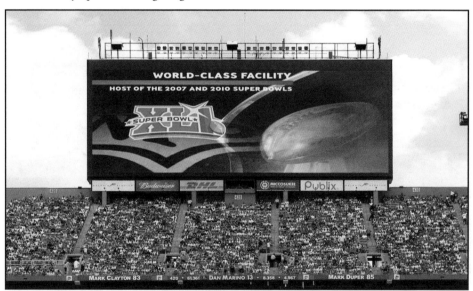

Miami Dolphin fans have two huge Daktronics displays to check out when not watching the action on the field. Dolphin Stadium is the only professional football venue to have not one, but two high definition displays with unbelievable clarity and definition.

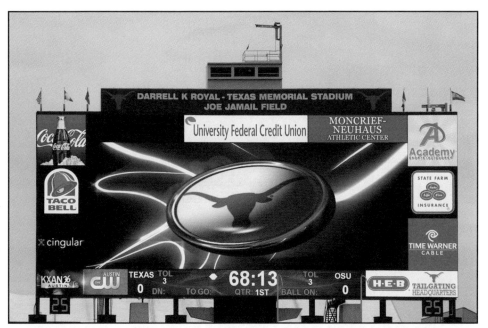

This huge Daktronics display at the University of Texas is known locally as Godzillatron. Over five million light emitting diodes make it the world's largest and one of the most spectacular anywhere.

Daktronics CEO Jim Morgan, left, and now-retired Daktronics engineer Vern Voelzke, use StarBurst® illumination being tested at the Brookings plant to check over design plans.

This Lehman Brothers display would be a traffic stopper in any city but busy New York, but it still catches the eye and impresses millions who marvel at what was one of the largest single Daktronics projects ever at about $16 million.

Daktronics has a presence in over 90 nations all over the world, including this 328-foot long display in the Kuwait Stock Exchange in Kuwait City.

The spectacular Grand Lisboa Hotel and Casino in Macao has an acre of lights designed and engineered by Daktronics. The LEDs are constantly forming computer-controlled, colorfully changing patterns. The project is evolving, with a hotel, to be highlighted and outlined with Daktronics displays, being constructed over and above this stunning acre of lights.

A scoreboard display for the Clemson University Tigers was one of the first big screen displays installed by Daktronics. It has since been moved to Clemson's baseball field, and a larger Daktronics display now graces Frank Howard Field.

Display sections for the Cleveland Indians main board are put through their paces in the Daktronics plant in Brookings to insure perfection when in place at Jacobs Field.

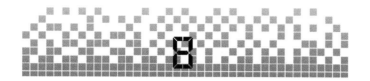

Going to the Mat

Responding to a classified want ad in the local newspaper for part time help, former country school teacher Faye Dahl was surprised that the business she was about to join was located in a little one-bedroom stucco house just off west Sixth Street in Brookings.

"The kitchen was the reception area and the manufacturing was being done in the garage," Dahl, who grew up on a farm near Astoria, SD, remembered from that first day on the job with Daktronics in September of 1970. Experimental work and testing was taking place on homemade work tables in the living room and in the bedroom of the home. "There

One of the first Daktronics employees, Faye Trapp Dahl, at work helping with the Utah electronic voting system.

were four employees working when I came in—and not a woman in sight." She later learned it was the fledgling firm's part-time secretary's day off. Dahl, whose youngest child had started school and given her more time, was taught how to solder wires for Daktronics' new solid state electronic voting system being made for the State of Utah.

The new Daktronics facility in the tiny house was necessary because the company had outgrown the 400 square feet of space in Orville Duff's Tire Shop. Now with 1,000 square footage counting the home's garage, the Daktronics manufacturing operation consisted of a few hand tools (some from Kurtenbach's limited home tool box), simple testing instruments, and a desk or two. But it was a start.

The Daktronics story started here, where the first production facility was located in one-half of the Duff Tire Shop in Brookings, SD.

Another new employee in the little house on First Avenue was lanky Ed Weninger. He was hired during his final year of study for an Industrial Electronic Technology degree at North Dakota College of Science and Technology. Kurtenbach drove to the Wahpeton campus to interview prospective employees for his new company. He had appointments to meet with three students, among them Weninger. As each interview ended, Kurtenbach invited the interviewees to visit Brookings and his Daktronics plant whenever they liked. Weninger, impressed with Kurtenbach had what he heard from about his dreams for the new company, made the trip south to Brookings one Saturday later in the school year, armed with the company's street address written on a small piece of paper.

He easily found 614 First Avenue, but when he nudged his car up to the curb in front of the house, he wondered if he'd found the right place. "It was just a little old house without a company sign out front or anything," Weninger said. He drove around town looking for another First Avenue. "I didn't find another possible location so I went back and knocked on the front door." Kurtenbach answered the door and invited Weninger in. He remembers the brownish carpet in the living room and the linoleum in the

102

kitchen. The bathroom had a bathtub that Daktronics technicians later used to develop its prototype printed circuit boards.

"We visited a while and then he asked me to ride along as he conducted some errands in town," Weninger remembered. They drove around in Kurtenbach's decade-old white Ford Falcon with the faulty heater. Kurtenbach pointed out the sights and then they stopped at the First National Bank (now First Bank & Trust) where Kurtenbach had business. The bank was next to a popular collegiate hangout, Horatio's, and Kurtenbach pointed that out. Weninger remembered that while he wasn't necessarily impressed with Horatio's, "I did think Al was rather astute in pointing out the bar to a young twenty-year-old bachelor."

At the time, Weninger was debating which of three job offers he would accept after graduating that spring. Salary offers? Kurtenbach had offered the least pay of the three. Still, Weninger was attracted to Daktronics. He liked the idea of a challenge. Joining a start-up company appealed to him. He was impressed with Kurtenbach's visions of what the company might become. Weninger thought it would be exciting to join a company that planned to build something from nothing and it was most definitely something I was interested in."

Weninger was eventually hired. "Actually, I wanted the job so badly that I think I pestered Al until he offered it to me," Weninger remembered. His first day in the little house on First Avenue was June 8, 1970, a day before his twenty-first birthday. He was assigned to an old work bench in the living room and put to work helping develop a digital thermometer the company hoped to market. Later, he worked on the first solid state electronic voting system, using the new electronics just introduced at that time by Texas Instruments. Then, Weninger joined a small Daktronics team developing a new scoreboard for

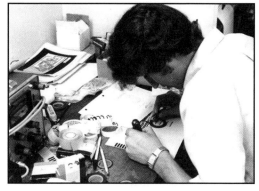

Veteran Daktronics employee Ed Weninger, at work in the early 1970s on the never-marketed electronic thermometer the firm hoped to develop.

the sport of wrestling. He was specifically asked to devise the board's solid state timer. He remained with the company, filling a number of important management slots, and is now Director of the Customer Service Department.

James B. Morgan, with whom Weninger was working, was an electrical Engineering graduate student who grew up on a farm near Luverne, MN, and graduated from high school at Ellsworth, MN. He was working part-time while involved in graduate work in electrical engineering at South Dakota State University. Kurtenbach was well acquainted with Morgan because he was Morgan's thesis advisor, and Kurtenbach asked him to help out at the plant when he could.

"I thought it was a pretty simple operation then," Morgan remembered of his early days with Daktronics. His early work at the embryonic company was helping Kurtenbach develop a heart training aid, a three-dimensional model that displayed the electrical stimulation of the heart. Kurtenbach's intent was to market the device to hospitals and clinics. "The entire operation then consisted of Al Kurtenbach and Duane Sander, a few tables, some test equipment, and some development work. It was a very simple and a very raw beginning."

Somewhat later during the formative, evolving years, Daktronics would also develop a system for weighing individual kernels of grain and computing statistical parameters on 1,000 kernel samples. Also, work was progressing in the late 1970s on a custom fire alarm for Bismarck, North Dakota. There would also be break-throughs on a sophisticated computer control system designed for the Brookings Waste Water Treatment Plant. That design was perfected in the late 1970s and installed in 1980, as was a similar system for the Yankton (SD) Fresh

Daktronics co-foundes Dr. Aelred Kurtenbach and Dr. Duane Sander huddle to work out a kink of their unique electronic voting system.

Before it discovered a niche in the sports scoreboard and display area, Daktronics engineers developed this one-of-a-kind central control system for the Brookings Wastewater Treatment Plant.

Water Treatment Plant. That first year, Daktronics had sales before expenses of $2,352. The company was still searching for its specialty and for its market niche.

Times were difficult. Daktronics' future seemed tenuous. But all this wasn't new to Kurtenbach. He was born during the Great Depression, made even more infamous because of the drought and dust called the Dirty Thirties. Then, the future always seemed distant, and dreams were shelved for the long hibernation of crops in the heat and hopelessness. Like everyone else, he'd rolled up his sleeves and waited out the difficult times back on the Dimock farm. He'd watched his parents survive the ups and downs of the farm markets. Something would break. Rain would eventually fall. Fields would turn green again. Forever the optimist, Kurtenbach never doubted success. He just knew that times would get better.

And they did.

Thumbing through the *Wall Street Journal* one day in May of 1970, Kurtenbach read of the Utah State Legislature's plan to re-call for bids for an electronic voting system. He read the story over again and again. "I didn't sleep that night thinking about the possibilities," he said. Up early the next morning, he wrote a letter to Utah requesting the system's specifications. After the specs arrived at the Daktronics office, Kurtenbach and Sander figured out what would be needed and how they would engineer their system. Because an unsuccessful bidding process for the voting system had been set aside two years earlier, Kurtenbach studied those bids before arriving at the Daktronics' cost estimate. "I guess being in education taught us that studying the problem was the best way to solve it," he said.

Once the system was designed, Kurtenbach sought out Milo Potas, a talented Brookings craftsman to devise a handy little voting system demonstration model that fit into a briefcase. With that in tow, Kurtenbach caught a flight to Salt Lake City to be there for the bid letting. Daktronics, with the first solid state electronic voting system ever designed, submitted the low bid of the three submitted. A lawyer for the company that had the next lowest bid argued on behalf of his client. He asked how Utah officials could think of awarding the job to an untried, embryonic, and untested little firm from Brookings, South Dakota. Loren Pace, Speaker of the Utah House of Representatives who was also the official in charge of the bidding process, had a perfect response. "Has your client ever built a first system?" he asked the lawyer. Daktronics' bid, because of the price of $87,875, the brief case model, the company's customer service plan, and the system's functionality, was accepted in July of 1970. It was an historic first step for Daktronics and Kurtenbach, the company's first exposure to the so called "outside world," remembered veteran employee and now Daktronics president and Chief Executive Officer James Morgan.

About this time, word of the formation of the little start-up company in Brookings soon came to the attention of South

The demonstration model of the first Daktronics electronic voting system for the Utah Legislature.

Dakota Governor Frank Farrar. At the invitation of the Brookings Industrial Development Corporation and the Brookings Chamber of Commerce, Governor Farrar, members of his staff and commissioners on the state's Industrial Expansion and Development Agency (IDEA) visited Brookings on November 4, 1970. Farrar and the agency were attempting to encourage development efforts in the state, and the visit was part of that pursuit.

Governor Farrar, a resident of Britton, still remembered that visit to the Daktronics "plant" and his tour of the little house on First Avenue. "In our travels around the state to promote new business we happened to run across Al Kurtenbach and Duane Sander and their new venture called Daktronics," Farrar recalled. "I was overjoyed during our tour of Daktronics and visits with Al and Duane to learn more about the concept and the courage shown by the two men." He said the state could not have asked "for a better

Dr. Aelred Kurtenback, left, and John Bibby, right, local businessman and president of the Brookings Industrial Development Corp., were at the Brookings Airport to welcome South Dakota Governor Frank Farrar, who toured the fledgling Daktronics plant.

business or more generous owners."

After Kurtenbach's guided tour for the governor, he and Sander continued to work installing the new Utah voting system. That work ushered in another "first" for Daktronics. Kurtenbach bought the first company car—a used Ford—to make travels around Salt Lake City easier during the installation process.

Vern Voelzke, now a retired Daktronics engineer, remembers that first company car well. By then it clattered back to South Dakota and Voelzke used it the rainy night he had to drive to nearby Carthage to pick up a voting system part being dip-soldered there. As he drove in the rain, he felt the front wheels planing on the water standing in the road. The car ended up in a ditch full of water. Voelzke got out as quickly as he could and hiked to a nearby farm to call Jim Morgan in Brookings for help. But it was Kurtenbach who eventually drove up to the farmhouse to get Voelzke. "This surprised me, and I also remember that it was a very quiet ride back to Brookings," Voelzke said with a smile.

With the car retrieved from the ditch, the work on voting systems and dip-soldering in Carthage continued. Kurtenbach's partner, soft-spoken Sander, remembered that first relatively large project for Daktronics that gave their company a new tack and helped open doors to other states planning similar systems. "We got that project because of an excellent sales presentation by Al, a briefcase-sized working model of the voting system, and a legislative leader who took a chance with a start-up company," Sander said.

Even today, if needed, Kurtenbach is ready to hit the road and help sell a Daktronics product. In the early years, he was the company's premiere salesman, and his philosophy of salesmanship remains today. Speaking of those early sale years, Kurtenbach said he went out to sell partly because of the lack of personnel to do that work. "And I think it's also important for the guy who runs the company to get involved in selling," he said. "Presidents who go out and get involved in the presentation give the customer confidence." Kurtenbach often told his company's younger sales staff that "selling is just another term for helping people."

As business improved, the small Daktronics crew moved out into the attached one-car garage at 614 First Avenue and went to work manufacturing and then installing their system, which was just what Utah legislators wanted. The task was completed by February of 1971. One unforeseen problem did cause some head scratching as the first Utah Legislative session was gaveled to order. Carpets in the Utah House caused a static disruption in the system. Until Daktronics engineers could alleviate that problem with a simple design change, a small amount of water was periodically sprayed on the carpet during sessions to prevent the static from building up to a disruptive level.

Four years after the first installation, the Utah House expanded its membership from 69 to 75. This meant a design change and a retrofit. But under the supervision of young Daktronics employee Giles Godes, the job was quickly completed for a fee of $4,000, about $800 more than the entire gross income of the company during its first year. Thanks largely to the successes of the Daktronics vot-

Top: Dr. Aelred Kurtenbach and Dr. Duane Sander with part of their first electronic voting system that was installed in the Utah Legislature.

Bottom: Giles Godes helped install Daktronics electronic voting systems throughout the nation.

ing systems, annual sales in 1971 reached a remarkable $242,550, an encouraging increase from the first year's $2,352 in sales.

The sophisticated technology of the Daktronics solid state electronic voting systems were tweaked and improved by engineers and technicians over time, but one aspect of the system required the artistic hand of Brookings inventor-artist-craftsman named Milo Potas. His day job was as a visual aids expert and builder of teaching aids for the South Dakota Cooperative Extension Service at the university. Potas had made the Daktronics voting system demonstration model into that valise Kurtenbach carried to show off the product to Utah officials.

Once the contract was signed with Utah, Kurtenbach asked Potas to do the woodworking, making appropriate control consoles for the desk of each lawmaker, and the more elaborate control consoles for legislative leaders and clerks. He also engraved names required for the Utah system and subsequent systems Daktronics would sell. At first Potas did the work alone, but soon Daktronics was sending help to his workshop. "Milo Potas was a true Godsend for Dakronics," Kurtenbach said.

Incidentally, Potas, who is a former Wentworth, South Dakota, farm boy, was a Signal Corps master sergeant who during WW II helped invent and design America's sequel to the German encryption and de-coding machine known as Enigma. The U.S. version Potas helped develop was called Sigma.

The year after Daktronics got the job for the Utah system, it was also successful in bidding a similar project in Montana, and Kurtenbach later heard of plans by the South Dakota Legislature to install an electronic voting system in the House of Representatives. He submitted the low bid of $63,000 to fill the bill. In due time, the Brookings firm received the go-ahead to install a $151,000 voting system in Illinois, followed by Colorado. Daktronics was becoming a high profile company making a name in the somewhat limited electronic voting systems market.

Kurtenbach and young Godes, armed with the demonstration model of the Utah system, represented Daktronics at the company's very first trade show, setting up a booth and plugging in the model voting system at the National Council of State Legislators convention in 1970 in Salt Lake City, Utah. It was the first of several dozen consecutive gatherings the company would attend to spread the word and show off its very successful voting system.

"In the 1970s and early in the 1980s, designing and manufacturing electronic voting systems provided us with cash flow to develop other products," Kurtenbach said.

Word spread of the practicality of the system and the impressive follow-up customer service offered by Daktronics. The South Dakota company continued to be the successful bidder in state after state, year after year. For example, within the first two weeks of January of 1975, six Daktronics-designed solid state electronic voting systems were "turned on" in the New Hampshire House, North Caroline Senate, Iowa House and Senate, Colorado House, and the Oregon House of Representatives. The New Hampshire House system included a computer as an integral part of its operation, an historic first in the industry of electronic voting systems.

The functionality of the Daktronics voting system which Loren Pace of Utah so appreciated, continued to impress others, as did the company's less obvious but important selling point called customer service. The customer service component was as aspect that Kurtenbach early on had insisted—demanded—be a part of every Daktronics product. He knew from his work on the Air Force radar equipment that proper maintenance helped add life to equipment, and timely response was important when trouble developed. Electronic circuits are not perfect, so failures do occur, and he was determined that prompt customer service be a company standard and basic policy. Today, Daktronics customer service remains unparalleled in the industry. It is a part of the company's culture and considered the responsibility of every company department and every company employee.

That dedication to customer service has been demonstrated many times. It is perhaps best exemplified by a problem that developed in the California Assembly's Daktronics voting system. At the request of the California Assembly, some changes and upgrades had been made at the Brookings plant to the software used in the system. The changes were sent to the California Assembly's voting system supervisor with instructions on how to incorporate the upgrade into the system.

The change was made near the end of the session when a day's agenda might include 150 separate vote tallies. On the day after the changes had been added to the system, there was a malfunction. It was a disaster. Voting tabulations had to be kept using a blackboard and chalk, slowing down the process of governance tremendously. Needless to say, leaders of the Assembly were not happy. Willie Brown, the Speaker, was insistent that Daktronics have someone there immediately to fix the problem. He even offered to send a California National Guard plane to Brookings to pick up technicians for a quick flight back to California.

But Daktronics made local arrangements, and Seth Hanson and Howard Jorenby flew by chartered plane to Sacramento, arriving about 4 p.m. The California Highway Patrol met them at the airport and, with sirens wailing and lights flashing, the two Daktronics experts were driven to the Capitol Building, arriving about 5 p.m. Within five minutes the cause of the problem was located. It was discovered that the Assembly employer had inserted the new software incorrectly into the system, causing the untimely breakdown. The system was soon back on line. Speaker Brown was happy, and the Daktronics tradition of customer service prevailed. Ed Weninger, currently director of customer service, lives each day with one major concern. "My biggest fear is that a piece of equipment is down someplace, with a customer frustrated, and I don't know about it." The Daktronics help desk is actually twelve desks in a phone center within Weninger's department, staffed at all times, day and night.

As Daktronics engineers, technicians, and workers became more adept at manufacturing the company's solid state voting systems, foreign entities joined the list of satisfied customers. A feather in its cap was the installation of a voting system for the United Nations headquarters in New York in 1989. During that installation, a small crew from the Brookings plant worked hand-in-hand with union electricians from New York. While the unionized workers ceased work daily at about 2:30 p.m., the Daktronics crew from South Dakota were just getting limbered up. They picked up the slack and worked far into the night finish the job.

Eventually, Daktronics electronic voting systems would be installed in forty Legislatures and Assemblies in thirty states. Also among voting systems with the Daktronics label were in the Yeman Parliament, the Nicaragua Assembly, the Albanian Assembly, and in the Parliament of the Czech Republic. Daktronics fulfilled a contract with the Lebanese Parliament in Beirut in

1995 with a $395,555 voting system.

By 2003, the somewhat limited market for electronic voting systems was resulting in an increasingly smaller percentage of business for Daktronics. So Jim Morgan arranged a "strategic alliance" between Daktronics and International Roll Call of Mechanicsville, VA. Under the arrangement, Daktronics agreed to discontinue further development of voting system software, and International Roll Call agreed to utilize Daktronics displays and discontinue its display manufacturing business.

Quite coincidentally, as Daktronics was developing the voting system market, a new market was finding Daktronics. And that's when another propitious opportunity presented itself. Probably because Daktronics was an emerging company just finding its footing, there was a certain youthful nimbleness that allowed for easy pivots from one product to another. And so it was from voting systems to wrestling scoreboards. The scoreboard proved to be the bellwether for the emergence of Daktronics into the world of sports scoreboards, message boards, and high resolution video display boards. It changed the course and the commitment of Daktronics forever.

South Dakota State University's wrestling coach, the late Warren Williamson, with an early Matside® scoreboard. It was Williamson's concept that resulted into the unique Daktronics wresting scoreboard that is still made today.

Much of the credit for the opportunity, Kurtebach said, goes to the late Warren Williamson, South Dakota State University's personable wrestling coach. Returning from the 1970 NCAA Division II wrestling tournament and in the planning stages for hosting the prestigious national event at his university in 1973, Williamson saw a need for a scoreboard specifically designed for wrestling. He served on the NCAA wrestling rules committee, was known as the father of wrestling in South Dakota, and knew the sport of wrestling. He arranged a meeting with Kurtenbach.

The two had first met when Kurtenbach's younger brother Frank was a tenacious heavyweight wrestler for South Dakota State University in the 1950s. At that time Frank encouraged Aelred to try wrestling at the School of Mines where Kurtenbach was earning his bachelor's degree in electrical engineering. Kurtenbach, always willing to accept challenges and try new things, accept the next challenge, knew nothing of the sport, but took his kid brother's advice. While he did not attain the high standing in the wrestling world that his younger brother achieved, he did make the Hardrocker wrestling team. With that wrestling experience, the Daktronics co-founder had first-hand, mat-side knowledge of the sport, and some ideas on how to devise a scoreboard dedicated specifically to the sport. Williamson had even more ideas on what was needed.

"Warren was aware that Duane Sander and I were in the early stages of starting Daktronics when he returned from that 1970 tournament," Kurtenbach remembered. The two men got together for coffee in the spring of 1970. Williamson explained his concerns about the lack of a scoreboard dedicated specifically to wrestling. "Al boy," Williamson said to Kurtenbach at that meeting, "the scoreboards they had down there (the national tournament) were just terrible." He said wrestling needed a better scoreboard, especially for tournaments when eight or ten mats are in use simultaneously in the gymnasium. The basketball scoreboards usually called into service during tournaments were cumbersome, blocked the view of many fans, and did not have capabilities for all of the scoring information. "Is that something you'd be interested in looking at?" Williamson inquired. It certainly was.

Kurtenbach was more than eager to lend a hand to create a prototype.

With Williamson's good ideas and suggestions, Kurtenbach asked young Daktronics employee, artist and graphics designer Dennis Holm, a native of Viborg, SD, to meet with Williamson. The two met at Cook's Café in Brookings and after discussing the current scoreboard shortcomings and the scoring needs of wrestling, Holm sketched out a rough design and shape on a restaurant napkin.

From that, he came up with a drawing to scale of the shape and configuration of what he and Coach Williamson had envisioned. They met again, made a few minor changes, and Holm, a graduate of South Dakota State University, then made the final scale drawing of the board. That resulted in the scoreboard shape, size and configuration that is still in use today. In the Daktronics archives is that first blueprint plan for the new scoreboard, signed and dated Sept. 16, 1970, by Kurtenbach. Holm, incidentally, went on to become art director of the Stamp Division of the U. S. Postal Service, Bethesda, MD. He is the same artist who created the famous Medal of Honor commemorative postage stamp that resulted in $24 million in sales to collectors and postal users.

James Morgan took those exterior design ideas and worked out the important mechanical, electrical, and electronic design. "The design and testing went well, and we all agreed that we had a product that would solve the dilemma for the sport and for the wrestling fans," Kurtenbach said. It offered improved features for crowd appeal as well as a functional value to wrestling participants, coaches, and officials. The very first, historic on-site testing of what the company dubbed the Matside® was at a dual wrestling match between South Dakota State University and the University of Minnesota, Mankato in, "The Barn" on the South Dakota State University campus in February of 1971. Kurtenbach wanted to be involved in the test and volunteered to operate the new board. "I learned I wouldn't be a very good scorer," he joked. "I kept forgetting to start the clock." Other than the inexperience of the scorekeeper, the Matside® worked perfectly.

One section of the pyramid carried the match score and the advantage or riding time. This section could be coordinated and used in conjunction with a traditional basketball scoreboard if necessary. Another section carried the time expired during a match. A third section showed the team meet score. Later, another section was added to show the weight division of the match in progress. It was a simple, ingenious, attractive yet functional design that could be manufactured fairly easily. It had a small footprint, and because it was in sections, a school could purchase the sections separately over a period of time as funds were available.

The seventy-seven by-forty-eight inch scoreboard was mounted on rubber casters friendly to gymnasium floors. It weighted only two hundred pounds, making it highly portable. It could be rolled out of storage by one person for easy placement at mat side. No special electrical power hookups were necessary. Another, still smaller section that could be added to the top of the scoreboard could carry commercial advertising messages, which could be sold by the purchaser of the scoreboard. The income so derived could then be used to help pay for the board, or to pay all of its costs over time. This melding of sport to business advertising to finance the scoreboard or raise income from athletic programs would become an integral part of one of the financing plans Daktronics' included in all of its future marketing of sports scoreboards and message boards.

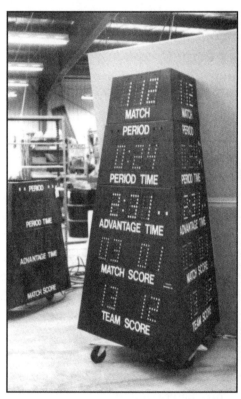

The Matside® had such an impact on the future growth of the company that it is still a company icon. In the main lobby of Daktronics today, displayed for all to see and to underline the pride the company had in that first big sports product, is one of those early prototype wrestling scoreboards.

The goal was to have seventeen Matside® scoreboards ready to use as demonstration models. They would be used at various 1971 collegiate and high school wrestling tournaments around the country to introduce the scoreboard and Daktronics maximum exposure to the wrestling

The first Matside® scoreboards were fabricated under the curved roof of a former feed supply store in Brookings, SD.

Ed Weninger, now Daktronics CEO James Morgan, and Brent Berger, were just getting started at Daktronics in the early 1970s, and worked to develop the company's very successful Matside® wrestling scoreboard.

community. Paul Espeset, Ed Wininger and others—including student interns— teamed with Morgan on the project. More space was needed for manufacturing, so an old, empty feed store, Hubbard's, on south Main Avenue in Brookings was rented. That space, and a building in the nearby town of Volga rented from the Volga Cooperative Creamery, expanded the Daktronics production plant significantly to 8,000 square feet. "But it was not a good configuration for a manufacturing company," Kurtenbach remembered. "It was cumbersome."

Faye Dahl, whose career at Daktronics started in 1970 when she was a part-time employee soldering parts for the firm's voting systems, was called back to help on the Matside® project. "It was very cold in the sparsely heated warehouse-type building we worked in, and I wore snow boots all day during the winter," she remembered. To add further challenge to the task, the building's water pipes frequently froze. "The pipes wouldn't thaw out until about noon, so no one could use the rest rooms all morning." She also remembered the cumbersome, huge wooden shipping crates they made to insure their precious new machines were not damaged in shipment to the various tournament sites. "They were sturdy, and I think they weighed twice as much as the Matsides they were protecting," she said. "But we were learning."

Kurtenbach remembers giving considerable thought to the manner of product packing for safe shipment. "We purchased a refrigerator for our home and I told the delivery people to leave the it in its shipping box," Kurtenbach said. "When I got home that night I unpacked it myself to see just how it had been prepared for shipping." Kurtenbach also spent time in the back room of Tom's Television in Brookings, watching and helping the firm's employees unpack television sets. From what he learned about refrigerator and television packaging, he was able to devise a reasonable crating method for Daktronics products.

Current Daktronics President and CEO Morgan also remembered the hectic times at the old feed store making and shipping the Matside®. "Our

The first Matside® scoreboards were fabricated under the curved roof of a former feed supply store in Brookings, SD.

118

first big purchase of metal working equipment was a power hacksaw from the Coast to Coast Hardware Store just down the street that was used to cut aluminum angles to make the scoreboard frames," he said. The late Brent Berger was hired as the company's first "chief saw operator," Sencore of Sioux Falls fabricated the sheet metal parts, and Morgan remembered how impressed he was when a Sencore engineer came up with what Morgan considered a "very clever method of fastening the three faces of the board together without the use of screws or rivets."

Morgan also remembered the pride he felt as he watched over the Matside® scoreboards at a wrestling tournament at the Naval Academy in Annapolis, MD, in early 1971. Kurtenbach was also busy escorting the scoreboards to various tournaments that Daktronics offered to service at no cost. Driving the Kurtenbach family's used Mercury station wagon that pulled a U-Haul trailer, Kurtenbach was just another company driver on many of those trips. On some trips, his wife Irene went along to help. Of course, the next day, back at South Dakota State University, Kurtenbach had classes to teach as well as a company to manage.

As orders came in and production went forward, Kurtenbach, often with the help of Williamson, traveled the nation on a killer of a travel schedule, visiting the colleges and universities who would be hosting tournaments, and stopping at other schools and colleges on the routes. "I have my

To promote the newly developed Daktronics Matside® wrestling scoreboard, it was provided free to several national collegiate wrestling tournaments.

119

wife to thank for caring for our home and for the children during the days and weeks that I was traveling," Kurtenbach said. "It was a very hectic time."

Mimeographed payment plans (the top-of-the-line Matside® sold for $2,520 cash or three annual payments of $922.32) and simple brochures were among mailings that went out to colleges and high schools everywhere extolling the virtues of the Matside® and the company's customer service.

Kurtenbach's forays into the gymnasiums, locker rooms, and offices of athletic directors and wrestling coaches around the nation was made so much easier, and he feels he was welcomed with more open minds, because of his affiliation with Warren Williamson, who was highly regarded and respected in national wrestling circles at both the high school and collegiate levels. "It was because of Warrren's influence that we were able to get this nationwide exposure in the initial year of the product's existence as we worked with our meager budget at that time," remembered Kurtenbach.

Daktronics was soon providing its three-sided, patented scoreboards specifically for wrestling to schools throughout the nation. Kurtenbach and

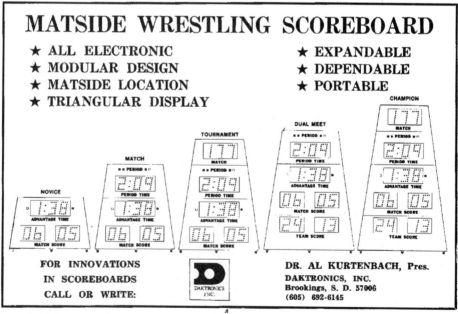

An early Daktronics advertisement in the 10th annual NCAA college wrestling tournament at Oswego, NY in 1972.

the others at Daktronics, as well as Coach Williamson and everyone in the Athletic Department at South Dakota State University, felt a particular pride when the 1973 NCAA Division II national tournament in Brookings used the new Matside®. "It was a great thrill for me to see them at work in the brand new Jack Frost Arena in March of 1973," Williamson said. He considered the new scoreboard "the breakthrough that advanced wrestling prominence on the national scene."

Wrestlers loved the Matside® because they could view it from the mat while competing. Within months, Daktronics had received over fifty orders for the truncated, three-sided boards. Two of the first high school customers for the new Matside® were Westfield High School in Westfield, MA, and Watford High School in Watford, ND. Both received their new scoreboards on February 2, 1973. The first high school in South Dakota to order a Matside® was perennial wrestling power Groton (SD) High School. Daktronics soon followed with a family of Matsides of varying sizes, one and two sides, and a table-top model, but the bigger "Championship" model proved to be the most popular.

It was the experience gained in the design, production and marketing of that first sports scoreboard that would point the way for Daktronics into the emerging market at sports venues. The Matside® gave the company momentum, and it gave Kurtenbach and the others confidence that Daktronics could compete. And finally, Daktronics was getting exposure and learning the proclivities of working in that broad and varied market that was invaluable in its future scoreboard ventures. "I am forever grateful to Warren for introducing us to the world of scoreboards," Kurtenbach said.

The Matside® popularity was most certainly a shot in the arm for the new company's bottom line. By 1972 Daktronics had 32 employees and annual sales of $352,000.

Another sports-related item that was more a curiosity piece than it was important and integral to the sports market was designed by Kurtenbach and others at Daktronics. At the time, South Dakota State University played its basketball games in what raucous students and other fanatic fans called "The Barn." It seated—squeezed in might be a better word—about 2,500 slim spectators, and its curved roof shape seemed to amplify crowd noise. It was often difficult for then Coach Jim Marking, who like Kurtenbach was a graduate of Parkston High School, to communicate with his players during time outs. They simply couldn't hear him because of fan noise.

So Kurtenbach and Marking devised a "walkie-talkie" system of sorts. Using a small microphone, Coach Marking talked to his players, all of whom put on headphones and gathered around him. It was used for the first time in February of 1971 at a loud game against the University of Northern Iowa with decibels bouncing off every roof board in the gym. Coach Marking's team, perhaps because of the clear, electronically delivered strategy, won 95-72. The coach used the system for several more games, but determined it was more productive for him just to yell instructions to the players rather than take the time for everyone to hook on to the electronic walkie-talkies.

In 1972, flush with the impressive Matside® successes and pleased at finding its market niche in the "go go" electronics business world, Daktronics adopted the theme "Scoreboards for all Sports." From this emerged other products that comprised Daktronics AllSport® line that was the most complete line of scoreboards available anywhere.

"We decided if we could do scoreboards for wrestling we could do them for other sports, too," Kurtenbach said. So Daktronics set to work manufacturing standard scoreboard models and timing devices that they called their "catalogue" models. An outdoor baseball scoreboard at Ervin Huether Field at South Dakota State University was the first venture into the outdoor scoreboard venues. There seemed no end to scoreboard possibilities. By 1975, the company produced a catalog of standard scoreboard models for dozens of sports uses, most for the traditional events such as baseball, football, and basketball, but specialized items followed for such events as Taekwondo, cricket, roller derbies, swimming meets, track and field, and even a scoreboard that it rented annually for the National Wild Turkey Calling and Owl Hooting Championships.

Daktronics wasn't concentrating only on the sports market. It was seeking other markets, too. Always the visionary and imaginative dreamers of new concepts and new uses for electronic products, Kurtenbach and Sander decided to enter the time, temperature, and message/animation business. It was a logical next step. The solid state circuitry and incandescent lamps of the voting systems and the Matside® fit nicely into development of that type of information signage for financial institutions, shopping centers, motels, stores of all types, and civic centers and similar public events buildings. Those first time and temperature displays were crude by today's standards, but they were the prototypes of today's more

The first Daktronics time and temperature display, Dakota State Bank, Milbank, SD.

sophisticated message boards. Remembered Kurtenbach: "We used lamp bulbs back then—a lot of lamp bulbs—and also, that was long before personal computers were introduced, which made display controller design a difficult challenge."

But they stepped boldly into this breach. During testing of prototypes in the time and temperature effort, a photographer from the local newspaper was on hand for the first test of a system in December of 1972. The temperature appeared digitally as planned. The problem was, it displayed a reading of 70 degrees, something unheard of in Brookings, South Dakota, in December. Shivering technicians soon discovered that the system had not been sealed adequately, and a sparrow had found shelter inside the system and built a warm nest next to the temperature sensor.

The first Daktronics time and temperature display was installed at the Dakota State Bank in Milbank, South Dakota. This was followed by the firm's first message center at the First Federal Savings in Devil's Lake, ND. During the 1970s, 1980s and most of the 1990s, Daktronics' systems used incandescent lamp technology before switching to what is now almost an exclusive use of light emitting diode (LED) technology.

Glen Robbins, who moved with his family back to his home state from Oklahoma, joined Daktronics in 1976 as an installer of the time and temperature systems. After a week of travel with his supervisor and a week in the plant to become familiar with the system, he was sent out on his own for an installation job. "I remember asking the bank president where the sign was to go," Robbins remembers. The banker responded, "You're the expert, you tell me." Robbins admitted his knees were shaking, but he selected a spot for the system and all went well. With each new contact, his shaking knees quaked less and less.

In 1973, the company organized a sales force to sell its products to schools and banks in ten upper Midwest states. This system of sales contacts continued until the end of the

Another Daktronics time and temperature displays.

decade when it was abandoned and separate dealer networks for high school and the commercial market was initiated. In 1973, 189 scoreboards were ordered. By 1977, that number surpassed 375.

Because of the work load, Daktronics for the first time initiated two eight-hour shifts. Before that, dedicated workers just responded to the work load and devoted longer hours in order to complete the job. That worker dedication took many forms. Retired farmer Ken Granum, who joined the firm in 1978, remembered that he brought his grain scoop shovel to work one winter to dig sheet metal out of the snow banks near the plant, where it was stored.

One of the benchmarks at Daktronics through the years has been that time and again, an individual accepts responsibility, usually without being asked, and steps forward to solve a problem, exceeding the employees' own expectations.

As the South Dakota sparrows of the winter of 1972 fluffed their feathers and awaited 1973 and the warmth of that new spring, it appeared as if Daktronics was on the verge of success.

But that wasn't necessarily so.

Kurtenbach considers 1973 as the company's most difficult.

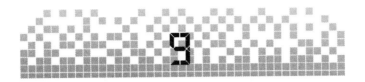

Great Timing

In the early 1970s, with the success of the Daktronics electronic voting system, its groundbreaking venture into the sports arena with its ingenious scoreboard for wrestling and other sports, and its growing message/animation systems for businesses and other uses, the company outwardly appeared to be on the cusp of success.

But the times were difficult.

The voting system's acceptance had allowed the company to increase employees numbers to meet production demands, but the scoreboard design and other costs, including the Matside®, left little in the Daktronics coffers. "There were a number of times when it was quite difficult to make payroll, but somehow we always did," Kurtenbach remembered.

This lack of cash, coupled with the need for more production space, was a nagging problem. "Our most difficult year had to be 1973," Kurtenbach remembered. Annual sales dropped to a third of what they had been in 1972 when orders reached the $352,24 mark. Orders for the Matside® were spotty during its introductory period, and the voting system business was also on-again off-again. Hirings and layoffs as the feast or famine flow of orders increased or decreased caused hardships for employees.

By the time those first seventeen Matside® scoreboards for demonstration uses had been fabricated, Daktronics had moved from the little stucco house and had also left the chilly confines of the old Hubbard Feed Store with its frozen pipes. The company moved to a 10,000 square foot, cement block building behind the Bunny Wash Laundromat, both owned by the Moriarty Family. It was a good building for Daktronics and was at an excellent location adjacent to the university campus and a block from Crothers Engineering Hall where Sander and Kurtenbach taught. "We could walk back and forth between our work on campus and at Dakronics, and it was very accessible for students who were employed," said Kutenbach.

Entrance to the third Daktronics manufacturing facility adjacent to the South Dakota State University campus.

But the building soon became too confining for all of that, of course. Kurtenbach had also rented the former Volga Cooperative Creamery building in nearby Volga for a metal shop. "All in all, this hodge-podge was not working very well," remembered Kurtenbach. "We needed to be all together."

As the Matside® scoreboards were being made, promoted and marketed, Daktronics also began fabricating standard scoreboards for other sports, including football, baseball and basketball. The metal work for the boards, after they were finished at the Volga site, were trucked the seven miles back to Brookings where the wiring and other components were installed. Some of the scoreboards being made were too big for the building so the work was done outdoors in the alley.

The standard scoreboards were of varying sizes, with the largest football scoreboards about fifteen feet long. Ed Weninger, now the Daktronics customer service director, remembered how he and Faye Dahl teamed together to twist red and black electrical wires together by attaching them to a power drill as they worked on the system in the alley behind the plant.

Howard Jorenby, another early employee who worked at the Volga metal shop, recalled one marathon session he had doing the metal work for basketball scoreboards. "I punched faceplates for the production run during a 25-hour period with one short sleep period in the middle of the run," he said.

Vern Voelzke, a mechanical engineer who joined Daktronics in 1971 and is now retired, remembered the Brookings back alley production line, too. "We had lights strung up among the tree branches, and we fought off mosquitoes. Cans of repellent were important tools in our tool boxes," he said. Kurtenbach often rolled up his sleeves, doused himself with mosquito repellent, and pitched in to help, too. Voelzke remembers going to the plant one Sunday afternoon, and being surprised to find the company president, Kurtenbach, pushing a broom, sweeping the plant floor. Kurtenbach said he often did some of the custodial work to allow time off for other employees. On many Sundays the cleanup became a family project, with the Kurtenbach children pitching in.

There was nothing visually fanciful about the scoreboards that Voelzke, Weninger, Dahl and the others were fabricating, although they did have solid state circuitry. Kurtenbach believes that the company's early introduction designing and fabricating those scoreboards provided experience and helped instill a "can-do" confidence in the minds of the young Daktronics

One of the first football scoreboards developed by Daktronics, undergoing final tests before being installed for the Aberdeen (SD) Golden Eagles. This scoreboard sold for $2,110 in the early 1970s.

engineers and technicians. There was also invaluable experience in the promotion and marketing of the boards and all of this would prove valuable for the next giant step the company would take in the late 1970s and early 1980s.

For the time being, however, Daktronics was desperately in need of larger production facilities. Working capital was also needed to provide for more inventory and to finance the firm's accounts receivables. "But we had no collateral to secure a bank loan, so it was a really very difficult time for us," Kurtenbach said.

The unblemished reputation of co-founders Kurtenbach and Sander and the manner in which they had managed their new business found a sympathetic admirer in the Sioux Falls office of the Small Business Administration.

Lyle Benson's job was to evaluate and assist emerging entrepreneurs in establishing new businesses and maintaining existing ones. He took an interest in Daktronics. "I met with Al Kurtenbach one day and he showed me a prototype of the wrestling scoreboard he wanted to produce and sell," Benson remembered. "His needs appeared to be simple, just some working capital and funds for construction of a building." But with no financial or business history to speak of, Benson had to decide if he should recommend approval of a significant SBA loan based merely on the character of Kurtenbach and Sander.

Reviewing the background of both men, Benson was not surprised to learn that both were respected in the community and dedicated and competent in their university teaching and research responsibilities. And from a cursory review of what the two had accomplished in the formation of Daktronics, Benson also determined that both Kurtenbach and Sander were "very hard workers."

Benson said he also sensed that both Kurtenbach and Sander were visionaries and fearless of the future. Like their pioneering grandparents, both were pathfinders in a new, emerging technology. "It was my conclusion that they had the personal characteristics that were needed and they would take on any challenge that came before them," Benson said.

The SBA loan that Daktronics was pursing required that a measure of financial assistance also be forthcoming from the community. The Brookings Area Development Corporation, then under the leadership of the late John Bibby, was organized to help emerging, deserving local businesses. So with its help, the SBA loan was approved. It made possible the first 14,000 square foot building at the plant's current site in east Brookings called Daktronics Park, on twenty acres of land purchased from dairy farmer David Gilkerson. Kurtenbach said the 1974 loan also provided adequate capital to carry the fledging company through its most difficult time. The building, constructed by the Mills Construction Company of Brookings, had adequate space to carry the company through into the late 1970s.

Taking part in the dedication of that new building were local and state officials, including Lyle Benson of the Small Business Administration, Robert Martin, director of the industrial division of the state Department of Economics and Tourism, Brookings Mayor Orin Juel, South Dakota Governor Richard Kneip, Roger Prunty, president of the Brookings Area Development Corporation, and Oliver Gottschalk, local businessman who was the event's master of ceremonies.

At that time, officers and managers at Daktronics included Jim Morgan, Systems Division manager; Vernon Voelzke, Time and Temperature manager; Brad Dawson, Scoreboard division; Brent Berger, project engineer; Giles Godes, assembly and installation supervisor; Jim Lambertz, supervisor of district sales; Patrick Schwan, manager of customer service; and Edward Weninger, customer service manager. At the time of the move into the new building in Daktronics Park, the firm had 40 employees and sales that in 1974 of $261,118 in sales.

The year before the 14,000 square foot plant became operational, an important and historic change took place within the Daktronics leadership. Kurtenbach and Sander decided in 1973 that because of the time required to manage the growing business and to market its stable of products, it was appropriate for Kurtenbach to resign his university teaching position and devote all of his time to the company.

Co-founder Duane Sander elected to remain at his teaching post, but he continued to advise and be involved as his time allowed. Sander said that he enjoyed the day-to-day and long-range challenges presented by the new business, but he also enjoyed the challenge of teaching. "I liked to have my fingers in the business, but I really didn't think you could run the show

Work on an addition to the first Daktronics facility in Daktronics Park in east Brookings, winter of 1977-78.

with two leaders," he recalled. "Al was really the brains and the salesman. I trusted what he was doing because I saw him when we were starting. I understood that he would not let the company go down. He would put out a superhuman effort to make it successful."

With full-time leadership, Kurtenbach first set out to departmentalize the various company entities, organizing around the product categories of voting systems, scoreboards, and time and temperature displays. Daktronics was now becoming more corporate-like and Kurtenbach was tireless in his efforts. A short week for him was sixty hours, a long week was seventy hours or more, and neither of these figures included travel hours away from home visiting with new or potentially new customers.

By 1977, the company reached a significant milestone, topping $1.17 million in sales. Two years later, in 1979, the number of Daktronics employees surpassed 100. Annual sales were nearly $3 million. With that growth, the new digs were again proving too confining for the increased activities. In 1978, an addition to the building was again constructed by Mills Construction Company of Brookings, doubling indoor production space to 28,000 square feet.

The timing couldn't have been better.

As the company was finding its place in the business world, settling in for the long haul with the popular Matside® and other standard scoreboards as its bellwethers, the world of sports was undergoing a remarkable metamorphosis, too. Interest in professional sports because of television was surging, particularly in football, basketball, and baseball. These three major sports seemed tailor-made for television programming. With the built-in pauses and stops and starts in each of these sports—innings, outs, touch-downs, two minute warnings, time outs, and quarters and halves—television, by now mostly in color, was beamed out from satellites and then cabled to every nook and cranny of America. During those commercial pauses for the home viewer, fans on site mostly sat to await a return to the action. A huge fan base was being built. More people were becoming hooked on sports. When they could, many fans traveled on new interstate highways to attend games in distant arenas and stadiums.

America's love affair with athletics naturally filtered down to the colle-giate levels, and then into high school and elementary school gymasiums. Colleges and universities that had been whiling away the years in aging, lim-ited-seating stadiums and in 1930s-style fieldhouses built during the Great Depression by the Work Progress Administration (WPA), were being over-run with fans who had more leisure time on their hands and more money in their pockets than at any time previous.

Also, Congress had decreed there be equal access and opportunity in hither-to male only sports. Title IX legislation gave females an equal share. The personal computer was also gaining in popularity at this same time. For the young fans raised on a diet of television, cartoons, and computer games, animation was accepted, expected and was becoming easier to create with imagination, pixels, and a little panache.

The building boom of new sports venues was underway. The new ven-ues came with all the amenities architects could think of, from luxurious box seats to fast food outlets, moveable stadium roofs, and huge score and message boards to inform and entertain during the game and the other natural lulls in action. The later, of course, required a "wow-factor". Later, as technology allowed, video screens entered the scene with their huge, sharp images.

Advertisers and a world economy were at the same time searching for new mediums and new ways to catch the attention of the now-generation. And that advertising component to Daktronics' success brings to mind the truncated Matside®. Most institutions of higher education sturggled to pay for the Matside® and finding advertiser sponsors was one way to help aug-ment their limited budets. At the secondary education level, Kurtenbach, as a former member of the Brookings School District Board, knew that public schools had limited budgets and many needs. It would be an exception rather than a rule that the scoreboard would be purchased with tax dollars intended for classroom, library, or laboratory use. So Daktronics added space on each scoreboard that could be used for placement of advertising. The income could fund the scoreboard or some athletic program. That seemed to Kurtenbach and to Daktronics a formula that could be expanded to help pay for all of the cost, or most of it, for the more elaborate scoreboards of every kind, and it fit perfectly into what was happening in a big way in professional, collegiate and high school sports.

So because of Daktronics' 1970s experiences in designing, building and marketing sports scoreboards and its message/animation systems, and with its growing cadre of computer experts and a nearby perpetual font of able and talented young collegians at South Dakota State University, Kurtenbach said he and his colleagues came to realize that the scoreboard in a sports facility was second only to the game itself when considering the attention of the fans. Although Daktronics had a catalogue full of cookie cutter scoreboards that could be altered or tweaked to some customized degree, new technology was opening a door for even more spectacular scoreboards and message boards.

The large, custom-designed scoreboards and message boards, some as an integral park of a complete visual communication package, were considered by Daktronics engineers as being palettes for electronic artistry. It was a natural next step in the evolution for the company. "The venue has to

The first Daktronics message center was installed at Devil's Lake, ND.

put on a show that's more exciting than people can get watching the game on television in their living rooms," Kurtenbach believed. Daktronics decided it would design products and create software and other support infrastructures to help venue managers get that "hey, look at that--wow" effect from the fans. "Our job is to help them do that, and we take that job very seriously," he said.

With its experience in solid state electronic voting systems, timing devices and digital scoring mechanisms, and with its message board experiences, Daktronics was well positioned for what was about to happen. New stadiums, new arenas, new fields of play, and new fieldhouses, each new venue needed scoring and visual systems to serve a new, computer and television-influenced public. The systems needed pizzazz and a creative punch to entertain and to become integral parts of the sport without overriding the sport itself, and advertisers wanted a piece of the action, too.

In 1977, Daktronics negotiated a working arrangement between Seagull, Inc., and Alex Cheng, who was an agent in the United States at that time for importing Omega sports timing equipment. That arrangement was

One of the Daktronics scoreboards at is first Winter Olympic venue in Lake Placid, NY.

critical to getting the order for the 1980 Winter Olympics because that is how Daktronics was introduced to the project. So Kurtenbach in 1978 sought scoreboard contracts with the 1980 Lake Placid Winter Games. His Daktronics bid was successful. Daktronics would provide nine scoreboards for that prestigious event.

Another historic achievement for Daktroncis during this time was the technological advances exploited by incorporating a microprocessor in each Daktronics scoreboard console. This system, including an addressable driver with the display, was designed by Jim Morgan and the late Brent Berger. With it, scoreboard consoles transmitted a data stream to control the various scoreboard elements. Engineers realized that Daktronics could not have specialized driver circuits for every different scoreboard. A generic driver was the answer. "The addressable driver greatly reduced the amount of cabling required between the controller and the scoreboard from how it had previously been done, and along with the microprocessor, it revolutionized our product line," Kurtenbach said. The addressable driver could control up to 16 display units, and it proved to be a significant milestone for the company. Without it, the Lake Placid experience might not have been possible. The driver allowed Daktronics to enter the large scoreboard business where conventional scoreboard digits are incorporated with programmable information and animation displays.

"This and other advances made fiscal year 1978 at Daktronics a watershed year," Kurtenbach remembered. The next year, Kurtenbach's younger brother Frank signed on with the company as the sales manager of the Standard Scoreboard Division. That proved to be an insightful hire. At that time Frank was teaching, and was head wrestling coach and assistant football coach, at Lincoln High School in Sioux Falls. He arrived just in time to lend his talents, his knowledge of sports and his personality in more watershed years waiting in the wings.

Technology continued its unstoppable march, and what emerged in the years ahead dovetailed perfectly with what Daktronics was attempting to do. The decade that had started at low ebb for Daktronics was becoming a much smoother voyage with specific ports of call clearly visible in Kurtenbach's sights.

The timing for it all was perfect.

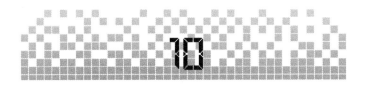

Olympian Efforts

...Enjoying the ski slopes and sledding hills of beautiful Lake Placid by day and dining on Dakota steak filets in the evening.

...Sampling Norway's famous marinated Edam cheese in Oslo, or viewing Manila Bay's fog-bound Island of Corregidor, The Philippines, from which General Douglas MacArthur departed for Australia in the dead of night during the alarming March days of 1942.

...Hearing the roar of the crowd and experiencing the ambiance of a football game in the famed Cotton Bowl in Dallas, Texas.

...Spending a loud New Year's Eve at Caesar's Palace in Las Vegas.

...Watching Tiger Woods calmly sink another impossible putt on an impeccably groomed green at picturesque Southern Hills Country Club in Tulsa, Oklahoma.

...Rubbing shoulders with the world's diplomats in the United Nations General Assembly Hall in New York.

Hundreds of young men and women from rural and land-locked Brookings, South Dakota, many who may have never wandered far from their home towns or family farms, did all of that and more during the remarkable 1980s and 1990s growth years at Daktronics.

But it wasn't all dining, sight seeing, and play, however.

In fact, there was very little time for that. Engineers, technicians, and other experts from Daktronics spent long hours working in the intense heat or the numbing cold depending on which of the world's hemisphere a new Daktronics system was being installed. They all may have been somewhat awestruck by where they were and what they saw and were involved in, but they set all that aside to make sure the company and the product they represented made a lasting impression on the world.

They showed that famed Daktronics employee pride. It was *their* product. They had helped to design it and make it and, by golly, it was going to work as they intended no matter what. In *their* minds, they *were* Daktronics. If a long drive to find a vital part was necessary, or a visit to sooth a concerned client or if an imaginative approach or a long night of retrofitting was the only solution, they were ready and willing. There were no whips cracking or supervisors issuing stern orders from headquarters back in Brookings, South Dakota. The comradarie of members of the Daktronics family in many ways personified the personality of its co-founder, Aelred Kurtenbach. "I'm not much for the old 'work ethic' adage," said Kurtenbach. "If you make the work interesting and challenging and delegate responsibility, you'll be surprised what people can do."

Al VanBemmel started at Daktronics in 1978 while a university student. A screen printer, he did many of the captions for the 1980 Olympic scoreboards but was not among those Daktronics employees assigned to work at Lake Placid to oversee installation of the scoreboards and to keep them operational. Still, he had a feeling of tremendous pride in his part in the Olympic experience. He remembers watching television at his home in Brookings as the United States hockey team fought its way to a surprise victory over the vaunted Russian team. He was proud of Team USA, but he also experienced a feeling of pride seeing the ice arena's scoreboard captions he had made displayed on his television screen.

The winning of the 1980s Lake Placid XIII Olympic bid for nine scoreboards caused people to sit up and take notice of this little up-start company from Brookings, South Dakota. Once people saw what Daktronics could do with its scoreboard technology, it set the company on a steady course and gave Daktronics broad exposure in the sports market. While that first Olympic contract may have put some strain on the personnel resources of the company, Kurtenbach believes the long-term effect of that first big international showing was beneficial to the company. The Lake Placid contract was probably not as significant a landmark for Daktronics as the Matside®, but it was certainly an important introduction to the world and set the stage for future Olympic involvement. "Lake Placid was a milestone event for the company," Kurtenbach said. "It expanded our marketing scope into the international field."

CEO James Morgan, who was the company's Lake Placid project manager, agreed. "It was a big turning point for us, and it gave us credibility."

Morgan, in his leadership role, supervised the design and fabrication of nine scoreboards for the Lake Placid event, as well as the necessary periphery elements, including the microprocessor-based computers that told the scoreboards what to do.

Morgan and other Daktronics engineers had by this time pioneered the use of modules, or display sections, that allowed the company to offer customers a range of both standard and custom products.

At Lake Placid, the Daktronics support crew lived together for over three weeks in a double-wide trailer home that Daktronics had rented. Many of the "family" meals came from a larder truck that Kurtenbach sent along. Included in that mobile pantry was a freezer full of South Dakota beef. Jim Anderson often took it upon himself to prepare the cuisine, which his teammates said was always an adventure. This practice of the entire delegation of Daktronics engineers and technicians living in a residential setting while working on large projects worked well and is a practice that continues today.

Often joining the cadre of Daktronics employees at Lake Placid was

This crew kept the Daktronics displays functioning during the company's first Olympic involvement at Lake Placid, NY in 1980. From left, Warren Stearns, Jim Anderson, Howard Jornby, David Gilkerson, James Morgan, Gene Long, Steve Lawler and Aelred Kurtenbach.

Kurtenbach, who suited up in the company's blue, monogrammed coveralls and worked side-by-side with them. He also made the trip a family vacation of sorts. His son Matt, now Daktronics' manufacturing manager, was ten years old at the time. Matt remembers that the entire Kurtenbach family journeyed to New York the summer before the Olympics as work was progressing on installing the Daktronics systems. Just as the memory of that family vacation is firmly etched in Matt's mind, his father, too, recalls the excitement of finally having Daktronics involved in such a prestigious event. It was at that time a highlight for the firm.

Daktronics really took off after the 1980 Olympics. But like most other businesses at that time, it also felt the sting of rising interest rates that were nudging up nationally to over 20 percent. Business slowed to a near standstill. To help pick up the slack, Kurtenbach hit the road, traveling the country nearly every week seeking to book orders of some kind. "Each time I returned, George Corvig, who was managing our manufacturing operation at that time, would meet me at the door with a quizzical look in his eye." More often than not there was no work.

Layoffs were common. It was not a happy time for Kurtenbach, who ordered his and all of management's salary reduced to help get by until things improved.

Fortunately, Daktronics was enjoying the glow from its showing at the Lake Placid Games. With a more aggressive sales effort, business began to arch by the end of the year. Employees were by now much more confident and experienced in designing scoreboards. "We'd get out a rule book for a particular sport and design a scoreboard to fit that sport's particular needs," Kurtenbach said.

With business improving again, the company decided in the mid-1970s to focus on display systems and abandon the other control systems it was working on. Kurtenbach still considers that change an important decision with far-reaching repercussions. The input of Jim Morgan, Kurtenbach recalled, was significant in reaching the conclusion that the company did. With scoreboard demand increasing, especially on the international scene in such places as Oslo, Norway, and in Manila, The Philippines, the workforce at Daktronics reached the 100 employee level.

The 1980 Lake Placid Olympics was followed in 1988 with a nearly $2

138

million Daktronics pres-
ence at the 1988 Winter
Olympics in Calgary,
British Columbia. With
that $1.7 million contract
signed, Daktronics sent
some of its engineers and
technicians with Lake
Placid experience to Cal-
gary, along with a cadre
of new personnel, to
learn the ropes and help
design seventeen custom

Daktronics display at the Calgary Winter Olympic ski jump venue.

displays. A challenge for this event was to include results in both English
and French and then interface all that with other equipment that had to be
engineered to perform under severe weather conditions. At that event, Daktronics provided scoreboards for every sport with the exception of hockey,
curling, and short-track speed skating.

For on-site maintenance at the Calgary venue, Daktronics purchased a
$90,000 duplex for use by the crew. A hole was cut in the wall between the
two living quarters transforming the duplex into a spacious eight-bedroom
home with four bathrooms and two kitchens. Fourteen sets of bunk beds
were rented from South Dakota State University and trucked to the home
to fill those eight bedrooms. Three television sets were set up in the house,
along with a VCR. During most of the time the games were in progress, a
crew of twenty-five lived in the house and enjoyed most of the comforts of
home, except for the cooking, which was usually catch as catch can or pea-
nut butter sandwiches. Seth Hanson was on-site manager of the Calgary
project, having just graduated with a masters degree in Electrical Engineering from South Dakota State University.

After the Calgary event ended, Kutenbach was pleased to share with
Daktronics employees a letter from the vice-president of Technology for the
XV Olympic Winter Games. "I wanted to record our great satisfaction with
the performance of Daktronics," John Russell wrote. "Our choice of Daktronics was based as much on the enthusiastic and flexible support of your

engineering and software people as it was on your price and flexible financial arrangement."

With endorsements like that, and with another Olympic experience under its belt, Daktroncis was becoming very good at competing for systems needed at international events. The company followed up the 1988 Calgary Games in 1994 at Lillehammer, Norway, and in 2002 with the Winter Olympics at Salt Lake City, Utah. It also had a presence at the Summer Olympic games at Barcelona, Spain in 1992, in Atlanta, Georgia, in 1996, in Sydney, Australia, in 2000, and in Athens, in 2004.

While Daktronics products were keeping the Olympic crowds informed, it was also building a considerable reputation at home in large scoreboard design, fabrication, and placement. In 1981 the company acquired Data Time swim timing assets, and this was incorporated into scoreboards specifically designed for competitive aquatic competition, which had a unique challenge because of the moisture-laden atmosphere in which it had to function. In 1998 at the Texas A&M Rec Center Natatorium in College Station, three world records, 13 American records and 23 U. S. Open records fell at the FINA Swimming World Cup and U. S. Open Swimming Championships. Daktronics systems worked perfectly. "The timing system was flawless and the meet ran without a hitch," wrote Don Wagner, head women's swimming coach at Texas A&M.

One of the first big scoreboards installed by Daktronics was at the famed Cotton Bowl in Dallas, Texas, in 1982. This was followed with an impressive four-sided display at The Omni in Atlanta, GA, that came complete with animation displays, a Sizzler® applause meter, stand alone shot clocks, and a Daktronics-designed courtside digital display scorer's table. With the up-tick in the need at sports venues, Daktronics could now provide custom scoreboards as well as standard scoreboards, commercial displays, and legislative voting systems.

While Daktronics systems were dressing up venues in ninety-five counties on six continents, the company was also shoring up its own house. Work started in the early spring of 1983 for a 36,000 square foot plant addition financed with $710,000 in industrial bonds issued by the City of Brookings.

Despite a light rain—never an unwelcome event in South Dakota—

more than 700 well-wishers were a part of the joyous ground breaking occasion. There to help turn a spade with Kurtenbach was co-founder Duane Sander and other dignitaries. Coinciding with the day on the grand opening, South Dakota Governor William Janklow declared November 19, 1983, as "Daktronics Day" in the state. With the new plant addition the company could now ship products six weeks after orders were received, placing the time frame in line with those of its competitors.

"It will be truly wonderful to have an overhead crane in the new addition, a real paint booth, and an indoor loading dock, among other things," Kurtenbach said at the ceremony. He noted with pride that the company had 150 people employed who represented 54 different South Dakota home towns. Also that year, stockholder equity passed the $1 million mark. Net earning per share was $5.70 and the company had record sales of $6.3 mil-

In 1983 Daktronics moved into new and larger facilities in east Brookings. Co-founder Aelred Kurtenbach turned the first shovel before others who helped in the growth of the company took their turn. From left, Faye Dahl, Ron Bjerke, Elmer Weiser, Aelred Kurtenbach, Dave Kosbau of Waltz Construction Company, Ron Einspahr, co-founder Duane Sander, Brookings Mayor Roger Prunty and South Dakota State University President Sherwood O. Berg.

lion. By the mid-1980s, the company was on firm enough footings for Kurtenbach and the leadership to offer to offer company stock to employees through an Employee Stock Ownership Plan (ESOP). This was in keeping with Kurtenbach's belief early on that each worker deserved a vested interest in the growth and profit of the company.

For Kurtenbach, the time had also arrived in the life of Daktronics to formalize long-range planning. Up to that point, long-term planning had been done mostly in Kurtenbach's head. "In those days I could stay on top of both product and market development." But Daktronics was outgrowing the "top of the head" planning. Kurtenbach decided that strategic and business plans would from then on be well thought out and well documented.

Some of that strategic planning had to do with the company's inventive development of what it called Starburst® technology. The historic first 16-color Starburst® display was produced in 1984 for the Edgewater Hotel in Laughlin, NV. The color in Starburst® was accomplished by painting the bulbs for outdoor use and by silk-screened filters for indoor displays. The colored bulb and filter technology was the only color technology that Daktronics had until 1989. That was the year that the company developed Starburst® use of lenses with light reflecting prisms. The first scoreboard to use this approach was installed at the University of Michigan. Daktronics engineers were able to improve and expand the technology and the new process carried it through many years. It was part of the display introduced at a gala New Year's Eve "turn on" at Caesar's Palace in Las Vegas, the company's first large matrix color marquee.

Other systems of the same genealogical family followed in far off places, including a Starburst® system at the Utusan Pearl & Dean Causeway entrance to Malaysia from Singapore, and display sys-

Daktronics sign at Caeser's Palace, Las Vegas, NV. It was the company's first large matrix color marquee.

tems in the United Arab Emirates, Hong Kong, Taiwan, Australia, New Zealand, Saudi Arabia, West Germany, Belgium, and Bermuda.

Kurtenbach considered 1986 a great year. Sales surpassed $10 million and profits were up fifty-eight percent. If that wasn't enough good news, the company acquired the new Glow Cube® technology that had been developed by Roy McGreevy of New Zealand. McGreevy's idea included a patented element able to rotated in the blink of an eye to show a black or a colored surface. The elements reflected sunlight and were lit by fluorescent light after sundown. The cubes required far less power than incandescent bulbs, and sparkled with a brighter visibility at angles of up to 160 degrees.

The Glow Cube technology helped make possible the involvement of Daktronics in the Professional Golfers Association Tour (PGA Tour®), the Senior PGA Tour®, and the Ben Hogan Tour, plus various outdoor Olympic venues. Daktronics also tried to extend the Glow Cube technology to other venues, too, but found it was most effective for the outdoor sports venue, where there was no assigned or fixed seating.

For the PGA tours, with Kurtenbach and Chief Engineer James Morgan personally involved, the company devised an ingenious scoring system. After attending several matches to get a feel of the crowd and the game, Daktronics engineers set to work. They designed four systems totaling of 52 scoreboards that were visible and useful to the crowd but unobtrusive to the event itself. Each scoreboard was programmed by an FM radio signal sent out from specially designed Daktronics control centers manned by Daktroncis and other technicians working inside semi-trailer trucks sited nearby.

Each of the 52 Daktronics Glow Cube scoreboards had a programmable area sixteen feet wide and six feet high that contained over 5,000 of the rotating, fluorescent yellow Glow Cube pixel (See photo in color section). Changes in each scoreboard were made with radio command from hand-held elements as golfers completed each hole. To be less intrusive while the golfers were putting, the information was not changed when players were on the green, and were then updated after the golfers finished putting.

Two systems of sixteen displays each were used on the PGA Tour and two systems of ten displays each were used on the Senior PGA Tour. Each system had its own control room in the front of a forty-foot moving van. The displays were loaded in the back of the van and transported from golf course to golf course. Each week one system for each tour was in use and the other system was in transit to the next site.

Daktronics engineers seemed to have thought of every contingency. They even worked in a way to protect the big boards in the event of high winds on the course. An anemometer monitored wind velocity and when a critical wind speed signal was received, the boards were lowered automatically.

Each scoreboard was also able to work its cluster of Glow Cubes for fifteen hours on a single battery. That battery was in a golf cart parked below each scoreboard. Everything worked to perfection. The golfing world was impressed. To this day, Kurtenbach considers the PGA Tour project a textbook example of what planning, creativity, and teamwork can accomplish. The cooperation between the company's manufacturing component and the engineering design department was exemplary and it was absolutely necessary in order to build the types of large systems the PGA Tour deserved, he believes.

Art West, director of the PGA Tour at Sawgrass, Florida, took the time to write to Kurtenbach in 1990. "…each of the 52 scoreboards was transported, erected and operated at our professional golf tournaments (over 70 events). The performance of the equipment was outstanding," he wrote. "We were particularly pleased with the software package developed by Daktronics, and the ongoing programming support provided. The fact that we purchased the scoring equipment for the new Ben Hogan Tour (30 events) is an indication of our satisfaction with Daktroncis," West concluded.

Daktronics workmanship and technological exprtise were again in the spotlight the day after April Fool's Day in 1987 when then New York Mayor Ed Koch, at exactly 6:52 p.m. Eastern Standard Time, hit the switch that fired up the famous zipper sign on the Times Tower Building. After a retro-fit by Daktronics engineers, messages again moved entirely around the Times Tower at a ticker-tape pace as if being typed out by an Associated Press reporter. It was that same zipper concept that had announced the successful election of president-elect Herbert Hoover in 1928, the United States entry into WW II in 1941, and other historic messages. It had fallen into sluggish disrepair and eventually was turned off until Daktronics revived the system.

Using its state-of-the-art central system, Daktonics engineers renovated and put the zip back into the historic message board. Kurtenbach and Daktronics service specialist Dan Bell were there for the "turn on" by Mayor Koch. After the much-publicized event, the two South Dakotans joined with the VIPs of New York at a gala reception at the famous Sardi's Restaurant in New York City's theater district. Although Kurtenbach enjoyed the party, he would have felt more at home sipping coffee at the Corner Café in Parkston where his mother Theodora.

The emergence of the LED, the remarkable, adaptive little hero in the electronics display world, helped bring about another sea-change for Daktronics. LEDs form the numbers on digital clocks, transmit information from remote controls, light up watches, and signal when kitchen appliances are turned on, for example. General Electric scientists had developed the LED's first practical use in 1962. Grouped together and controlled by programmed computers, LEDs can form images on a jumbo television screen or illuminate a traffic light. They are tiny, energy and space-saving light bulbs, but unlike the incandescent bulbs, they have no filament to burn out, do not get overly hot, and they do not easily break. Kurtenbach and other Daktronics engineers recognized, of course, the potential that the tiny solid-state devices held for their business.

A light emitting diode (LED) that has made possible today's unbelievable scoreboards and video displays.

So the company was poised to revolutionize the sports display industry by incorporating the LED technology in its scoring displays, programmable message boards, and eventually in their programmable video systems.

The same year that the LED became a vital cog in its products and its future growth, Daktronics was successful in the acquisition of companies with special expertise complimentary to what Daktronics was doing. Kurtenbach negotiated for the purchase of Star Circuits, Inc., of Brookings, a manufacturer of circuit boards. Also acquired was Chrondek, the motorsport timing company, which gave Daktronics a road-hugging grip in the niche market of auto racing, a sport that has enjoyed phenomenal growth.

Late in the 1980s, Kurtenbach and others in management decided to change the emphasis of the company from a product selling effort to one dedicated to serving customers in special markets. "This was another very basic philosophical change for us," Kurtenbach said. "I think time has proven that we made the transition at the right time for the company." Under this team approach, the five major departments within Daktronics, administration, sales/markets, marketing support and customer service, engineering, and manufacturing, all came together to the benefit of the customer.

By 1988, Daktronics leadership had decided it was also time for the company to establish sales and service centers at strategic locations in the United States. It had ventured into this expansive mode in the late 1970s, but that was soon determined to be a premature start and the company pulled back. Now, Chet Feil, owner of Scoreboard Parts and Service in Seattle, WA, and an enthusiastic Daktronics dealer, wanted to retire, and Daktronics decided it was time to look again at developing regional offices.

Marlo Jones, a native of the little town of Pollock, SD, was attending South Dakota State University at that time pursuing his bachelor's degree in Electrical Engineering Technology. He had worked for Daktronics as a student intern in customer service, and after graduation in 1986 as a full-time employee. He had worked with Kurtenbach demonstrating the PGA Golf scoreboard system to RJR/Nabisco. Jones had also been involved with Daktronics at the 1988 Olympics in Calgary.

Jones heard that that the company was considering the purchase of Fiel's Seattle business. Kurtenbach and Jones talked about the possibility of his being assigned to the satellite. Jones remembered that Kurtenbach suggested the two travel to Seattle to look the situation over. That eventually led to the assignment of Jones as its Seattle office representative and manager. "Our strategy was to service all brands of scoreboards and message centers in schools and when equipment needed to be replaced we could also provide that service, too, with new Daktronics equipment," Jones said. He remembered that Kurtenbach was personally helpful in suggesting ways to grow the Seattle business and he also lent Jones support when more experience was required to make a good business decision.

"Al always believed in having a good plan and having goals," Jones recalled, "and we all learned from him." Soon, other regional Daktronics

Marlo Jones of Daktronics was picked to start up the first Daktronics sales and service office in Seattle, WA, after the company purchased a retiring Daktronics dealer's business there.

managers were being trained by Jones and today, that very first Daktronics sales and service office in Seattle has a staff of ten personnel and Jones is district manager of the entire Northwest area of the United States. "This allows me to help others grow in much the same way as Al helped me grow," he said. Over fifty Daktronics sales and service offices and dealerships now operate in the United States, and there are also about half-a-dozen in foreign countries.

Since establishing that first regional sales and service office in Seattle, the company has also added dealerships for displays in commercial applications, and has greatly expanded the concept of on-site sales and service representation in the areas of high school and parks and recreation, commercial applications, and the transportation market. This progressive step during 1988, coupled with the addition of plant space to 84,000 square feet, prompted Kurtenbach to call 1988 "a banner year."

The year 1989 would also earn an even more emblazoned banner for the company. A Daktronics voting system was installed in the General Assembly of the United Nation's Building in New York City.

Software breakthroughs and improvements evolved into the introduction of Daktronics Venus® 2000 and 6000 message center controls, the forerunners of today's even more powerful systems. And the company stepped boldly into new market opportunities, including the highway and traffic market with transportation displays, and into the airport market, providing gate schedule and baggage displays, for example.

Daktronics also entered the gaming and casino markets. There seemed no end to the possibilities, and each new market complimented the firm's major thrust in the design, fabrication, marketing, and servicing of large computer programmable display systems. About twenty-five percent of Daktronics business was programmable displays for businesses, such as car dealerships, drug stores, grocery stores, banks, and other commercial businesses.

Juggling all this, rolling up his sleeves to help where he was needed, inspiring others with lunch room chats, leading the cheers and setting goals, Kurtenbach was tireless and relentless. He seemed never to rest. He considered his primary responsiblity as company president as that of keeping Daktronics in a growth mode. Second, he saw his job as one similar to that of a coach, being a role model and providing strong but caring leadership. His players, Daktronics employees were then and are now the primary asset of the team. He values their ideas and feeds off their enthusiasm, self-confidence and youthful initiative.

With all that going for it, Daktronics was on a roll. And the climb to the top of the industry ladder through the final decade of the twenty-first century was just beginning.

A Daktronics highway message display on the highway in Cumberland Gap, KY.

148

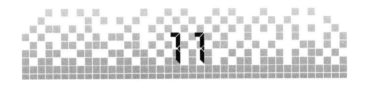

The New Beginning

Daktronics was fast becoming the shining star in the world of computer programmable information displays. One of its preeminent stars basked in the bright spotlight for the traditional Time's Square New Year's Eve salute as 1991 arrived.

A brightly adorned ball was poised to ascend to the loud cadence of the crowd's midnight countdown, but first, the switch was activated to bring light and movement to the wondrous Daktronics Coca Cola display for all to see. New York City was becoming a familiar gallery of Daktronics wonders and their now-famous "wow" inducers. Three years later just west across Broadway from the Coca Cola display, Daktronics installed a dominant Morgan Stanley display along the side and both ends of its new building. Kurtenbach considered that a "pivotal project" that happened before the bright blue light emitting diode had been invented. "Our design for the end wall displays on Morgan Stanley utilized the green and red LEDs with a full gray scale control system that produced an off-color video rendition," Kurtenbach remembered.

A Daktronics system had scored again. It was becoming commonplace for the little company on way out the flatlands of South Dakota.

The exciting journey for Kurtenbach and everyone at Daktroncis through that productive last decade of the twentieth century brought more innovations to its brief but storied history. The public embraced and loved every one of them. Daktronics was becoming synonymous the world over with expertise and innovations in visual communication.

Plant size at Brookings' Daktronics Park expanded, reaching 122,000 square feet in 1990. There were more additions by the mid-1990s until at the end of the century the plant complex was nearly 200,000 square feet. That would more than double with new plant space added in 2006—07. By century's end, annual sales leaned up against the $100 million mark. Sales grew in the 1990s at an annual rate of 19.5 percent. Profits were at an impressive twenty-six percent rate. Work force numbers grew like Harriet Beecher Stowe's Topsy, to 1,000 by 1999, including 340 part-time employees, most of whom were South Dakota State University students. Unbelievably, these measures of progress and success had not abated since 1968 when Daktronics first started out at a snail's pace in the west half of Orville Duff's little tire shop off Main Avenue in Brookings.

Kurtenbach credits much of Daktronics' success to a premise that he and co-founder and fellow electrical engineer Duane Sander established early on. They believed that at the core of any technology-based business was engineering know-how and product development. They were the vital linchpins. To help keep that spirit and tradition alive through the years, Kurtenbach made the decision as the new decade of the 1990s started that the company's cadre of inquiring, inventive engineers would be augmented by a supervised student shift in the company's Project Design department. Many of those students would become the company's future design engineers, he hoped.

He believed the company's ability to develop a solid, knowledgeable workforce was paramount. "There are no dumb questions and there are no final answers," he often told his university students and later his compatriots at Daktronics. In an era when use of overseas third-party vendors was common, Kurtenbach insisted that Daktronics design and fabricate all of its sub-assemblies and complete assemblies at the plant in Brookings. Some parts of the work might be done by other specialty businesses in Brookings or nearby, but Daktronics employees have learned to be multi-talented, devising new production methods and pitching in where needed, as Kurtenbach had learned to do as a kid growing up with farm chores back in Dimock. "Around here," Kurtenbach often said, "we are all just common, everyday people with uncommon motivation."

By the 1990s, Daktronics engineers and sales staffs were focusing their efforts on four major markets. The largest was the sports market division that was sub-divided into two groups. There was the large sports venues, where super sizing and custom work for large sports venues was the order of the day. A second unit concentrated on smaller markets, including most colleges, high school and elementary school scoreboard and message center needs, and the opportunities in what the company called the park and recreation niche market. Many of the scoreboards for these smaller markets were what the company referred to as "catalogue" scoreboards. About sixty percent of the Daktronics business was in this wide-ranging sports market that had started when ex-collegiate wrestler Kurtenbach and other engineers in the company perfected the Matside® scoreboard exclusively for the sport of wrestling. The company continues to manufacture this venerable, dependable and still stylish veteran that is now as common at collegiate and high school wrestling matches as the wrestling mat itself.

The third market pursued by Daktronics is in the transportation area. "As always," Kurtenbach remembered, "trying to penetrate this new market was a challenge." Daktronics decided to pursue three transportation areas: airports, light rail, and roadway displays. Kurtenbach and his team discovered that roadway displays had to be designed and built very differently than sports and business displays. But after some starts and stops and some reversals along the way, the company bit the bullet and learned what it had to learn. Now transportation displays are a significant and growing part of the overall business. A unique feature of the roadway displays, the market for which is primarily state Departments of Transportation, is that the displays are usually sited in isolated areas along roads and highways some distance away from control centers. They must be activated and controlled from afar by phone or radio communication. Daktronics now has message displays on many

A Daktronics technician doing maintenance work inside one of the company's big highway message centers.

A Daktronics message board at the Boston Tunnel.

major roadways, including New Jersey's Garden State Parkway, for example. Another big project in this division is helping out at what is known as the Big Dig, or the central artery tunnel through Boston, MA. Daktronics systems there are part of one of the the world's most advanced traffic-management and incident-response systems.

The fastest growing segment of the Daktronics market share is in the commercial-retail area that had been launched a quarter of a century previous by Daktronics' outdoor time and temperature/message displays primarily marketed to financial institutions. In the early days of time and temperature system development, Daktronics used lamp bulbs—box cars of lamp bulbs. And this was at a time before personal computers were introduced. This made display control a real challenge for Kurtenbach and his small cadre of design engineers.

After the successes of marketing the solid state time and temperature signs to banks and other financial entities, Daktronics assumed correctly that there were plenty of other potential commercial markets out there. It initiated an aggressive effort to introduce the marquee message and video displays to other segments of the retail business. Auto dealerships, shopping centers, convenience stores, drug stores, gas stations, and you-name-it types of retail businesses are finding that Daktronics signs help promote their businesses. The commercial-retail niche continues to grow with no sign of a letdown.

Although not promoted as heavily, Daktronics is also finding that churches and schools are discovering how message systems can be used to their advantage. For example, the huge Lakewood Church in Houston, TX, purchased three Daktronics ProStar® video dispays with a clearness, or resolution of clarity, to project images to an average assembly of about 16,000 church goers.

The commercial-retail sales and marketing effort is managed by long-time Daktronics employee Sue Almhjeld. She joined the company in 1976 when it had about fifty employees. "We were living day-to-day then," she remembered. "We were wondering—are we going to make it?"

As the century's last decade marched in, the company was relying mostly on incandescent bulbs, Glow Cubes®, and a few other inventive light producing systems for its scoreboards and message centers. A new lighting technology emerged in the 1990s, called the wedge-based lamp. These are basically the same lamps use in car tail lights. The wedge-shaped source was more energy efficient and also reduced the problem of lamps burning out. But the use and scope of Daktronics scoreboards was becoming more complex—and much larger.

In 1991, two big Daktronics scoreboards were installed at the University of Florida and at the University of Colorado. Daktronics had a presence at the All-Africa Games in Nairobi, Kenya, and later at the 1991 All-Africa Games in Cairo, Egypt. There, the Daktronics scoreboard was "commissioned" in sheep's blood in a traditional ceremony where a bleating lamb was offered for slaughter at the system's base.

Another industry eye-opener that year was the famed Coca Cola sign on Times Square in New York City mentioned earlier. It was considered at the time as the ultimate in a commercial system. But a newer Coca Cola system would take its place in 2004 that was even more of a spectacular engineering achievement. It would become a stunning industry landmark, a stunning legend. More about this later.

A huge display and scoreboard, the company's first major league baseball order, was installed in 1993 at Camden Yards for the Baltimore Orioles baseball team. The Orioles management expressed a desire to have several "extras" on the scoreboard that had never before been incorporated in a major league stadium. Management wanted to show "left on base" information, provide real-time scoring updates from other stadiums, and display detailed play-by-play accounts on demand. Daktronics competitors claimed that such things were not possible. But Daktronics engineers and designers accepted the challenge and developed the software and wherewithal to meet the team's needs. Because of this, and its aggressive marketing, Daktronics in the 1980s and early 1990s won orders to install over fifty minor league baseball scoreboards and was well on its way to becoming the premier scoreboard supplier for professional baseball.

There was, of course, a large Daktronics presence at the 1992 Barcelona Olympics, too. The Olympics and Daktronics were becoming synonymous, it seemed. One scoreboard behemoth at the Barcelona swimming and diving venues glistened with over 200,000 Glow Cube® pixels. That 1992 Olympics event was followed by a flashing—and flashy—display of Daktronics systems at the 1994 Winter Olympics at Lillehammer, Norway.

A patented Daktronics presence at the Atlanta, GA, Olympics was even more obvious to millions who attended or watched at home. Almost everywhere on the vast Olympic grounds saw one or several of the more than 80 Daktronics scoreboards and displays were at work entertaining and informing.

As all this was taking place at the growing company and around the world, a tiny powerhouse of a light source was piquing the interest of Daktronics engineers, particularly Reece Kurtenbach, Alered and Irene's son. He had joined the firm as an applications engineer after earning his electrical engineering degree at South Dakota State University in 1987 and after working in Colorado for four years. Kurtenbach remembers that his son "had the vision and pursued it." The LED was the first light emitter that could compete with the sun since the light bulb. It seemed to Reece Kurtenbach and other Daktronics engineers to be the next giant step in advancement of information and video system technology. Daktronics engineers had been experimenting with the LED potential even back in the 1980s. In the 1990s, the firm had perfected the bundling or module approach to put the "little lights that could" into manageable systems. These moduals were in turn married to one another in such a way so that giant video and data displays were possible. As Reece Kurtenbach had envisioned, the LED revolutionized the business of visually communicating data, words, and pictures with computer-programmable information displays. Even early in the 1990s, Daktronics was designing and producing new, but small, portable LED scoreboards, primarily for the grade and high school markets and for community park and recreation entites, and developing tri-color LED matrix displays. By designing control systems, the basic-colored LEDs could be manipulated into an unbelievable, unimaginable 4.3 trillion shades of any color the human eye could recognize. Daktronics, because of its design and development talents and techniques, was ready for the groundswell the light emitting diode would create.

By the 1990s, incandescent lamps and other light source technologies in sports scoreboards had about run their course. They were doing about all they could do for scoreboard glitz and glitter. A new product was being used, but it was beyond the reach of Daktronics. That was the cathode ray tube technology (CRT). It made possible big video displays in scoreboards and on message centers. It was the property of the industry giants such as Panosonic, Sony, and Mitsubishi. The CRT technology was expensive for the user, however, so it had limited use in only the largest, most lucrative sports venues. Although Daktronics was still selling more than its share of big scoreboards, it had to partner for the system's video display component with the giants from Japan. By doing this, Daktronics was probably missing out on one-half to three-fourths of the large scoreboard market share because of the CRT corner the competition had on the technology.

But Daktronics engineers were rapidly learning how to apply the LED technology to video displays, which provided a far superior, less expensive product than the CRTs. Daktronics was perfecting methods to incorporate the LEDs into their scoreboards and devising ways to control those little diodes with computer commands. By adopting this light emitting diode technology and teaching them to dance in computer-driven sychronization, remarkable possibilities were possible. And by coming up with unique and creative ways of embedding them with assembly line accuracy and speed into small modules about a foot square, each square containing sixteen rows and sixteen columns of red, blue, and green pixels tied to a circuit board, Daktronics could not only begin to compete in literally the same big ball-parks with Panosonic, Sony, and Mitsubishi, but the LED video displays were far superior. Almost overnight the CRT became an albatross on the technological sea, unable to find the up-drafts it needed to remain in flight.

Daktronics sales immediately took off. Between 1993 and 2000, annual sales quadrupled, from $30.5 million to more than $123 million. Activity at the Brookings plant was booming, too, with the first three installations of their new computer programmable video display product in college stadiums in 1995. By the end of the decade, Daktronics had created, sold, and installed 42 new scoreboard/video board displays, each having the desired "wow" factor. Professional sports managers were awed by the remarkable color and clarity of the Daktronics systems for the Dodgers, San Francisco Giants, Red Sox and dozens more. Professional football was also seeking out Daktronics representatives. That included the New England Patriots, where another South Dakotan, Adam Veniteri, whom Kurtenbach had watched kick extra points and field goals for the South Dakota State University football team on many Saturday afternoons, was helping to light up a new Daktronics scoreboard at the Patriots' Gillette Stadium.

Although the LED was becoming the cat's meow and the industry darling, Daktronics wasn't abandoning altogether its other technologies, which still had some limited uses in specific instances. But it was backing away slowly from the venerable Glow Cube® technology, along with its Starburst® and SunSpot® displays, with its low-wattage lamps, highly polished reflectors, and directive lenses. It's Venus® computer control software continued as an important element for the company, and Daktronics has continued to expand its software and firmware development.

By 1994, Daktronics had 553 employees, including 153 students working part-time. There were seventy-six full-time, trained engineers working with thirty-nine student interns enrolled in South Dakota State University's College of Engineering. The number of engineers has increased each year since. Daktronics has for years been known in the industry as the innovator of the industry. Its long association and partnership with South Dakota State University has been invaluable in the company's growth, Kurtenbach contends.

Not only has Daktronics provide SDSU students with extra spending money, hands-on training, and real-world experience in a corporate atmosphere, but the company has always been more than generous and encouraging to the students and to potential students that it employed. It offers special incentives for good grades, and goes to great lengths to adjust student work schedules to fit around classroom requirements. There are special student shifts, a unique tuition reimbursement program, and Daktronics scholarships have assisted hundreds of students through the years.

In 1992, one of those students, Reece's younger brother Matt graduated from the South Dakota State University College of Engineering and after a round of engineering tasks at the main plant, he became manager of Star Circuits, a subsidiary Daktronics had purchased to manufacture circuit boards in the late 1980s. Of that acquisition, Kurtenbach remembered that the company faced a steep learning curve to master the science of circuit card fabrication. "But we did learn how to make them and by 1992 we reached a break-even point at Star Circuits," he said.

In 1993, the elder Kurtenbach, recognizing the creativity and product knowledge held by Daktronics employees, initiated an Employee Suggestion Program. Soon, nearly 900 suggestions had been dropped in the boxes situated in the plant complex. Of those, 538 garnered $25 cash awards and the efficient work of Daktronics became even more productive and cost effective. Ideas are always encouraged from Daktronics employees no matter the grade level in the hierarchy. The suggestions that seem to have potential are implemented.

By 1994, Daktronics employees by department were 67 in sales and marketing, 33 in customer support, 115 in engineering, including 39 part-time student employees, 312 in manufacturing, including 81 part-time student employees, and 26 in administration.

When Kurtenbach and Sander founded Daktronics in 1968, they had promised investors that within ten years their stock would be tradable and have resale value. "It actually took us twenty-five years to reach that benchmark, but we finally made it," Kurtenbach said on the occasion of the first trading of Daktronics stock on the NASDAQ market on February 10, 1994. At that time, 1,325,000 shares of common stock at a price of $7.625 per share went on the public market. Response was very positive and four days later, another 183,750 shares were offered. Upon completion of the offering, there were approximately 4.2 million shares outstanding.

Gaining a listing nationally was significant to the company and important personally to Kurtenbach, a man of his word, who had made a promise to initial stockholders who stepped forward with trust and faith to put their money into a new company. "Going public fulfilled a promise and a pledge I had made to our early investors," he said. Being listed on the NASDAQ was also important because it allowed the company to pay down some of its debt and provided working capital, Kurtenbach said. All of this greatly improved the company's bonding capacity and opened the door for Daktronics to bid larger projects and to take on more installation responsibility at the job site.

In preparation for that initial public offering of Daktronics stock, Kurtenbach spent week after tiring week traveling the county drumming up interest with what he called his Daktronics road show. Although he was accompanied by representatives of a Minneapolis-based company, Craig-Hallum, which specialized in IPO preparations, the "road show" was classic Kurtenbach. There was nothing expensive, lavish, fancy, or flashy about it. He didn't lug along detailed overheads in full color, or use bells and whistles to talk about what he had helped to create. He used his pleasing personality, his infectious enthusiasms and the "Kurtenbach from Dimock" down-home persuasive talents, augmented by a simple flip chart with a few colored slides and photographs of Daktronics installations, and a brief slide show, to tell the amazing success story. His presentation theme was "Setting New Standards Worldwide." And that's just what Daktronics was doing, and that's what made its stock very much in demand during the IPO period.

As the decade of the 1990s and the century were ending, another Daktronics star was capturing center stage. It was the advanced Venus® 7000 computerized controller, a vastly improved version of the first controllers invented by Daktronics. Kurtenbach considers the Venus 7000 a "breakthrough," opening the gates to smaller stadiums and arenas that were ready for video replay and other video uses. ProStar®, with the Venus7000 providing the brainpower, uses green, red, and blue light emitting diodes and mixes them on command with all the shades and hues and intensities of light that can be reproduced, numbering more than four trillion colors.

The Venus system harnessed to the magic of the LEDs made video screen displays almost clearer than the proverbial bell, and brought display screens to vivid life as never before. The results were spectacular, and they would become even better as Daktronics developed more expertise. The new outdoor system was first unveiled at football venues in Norman, OK, Clemson, SC and Pullman, WA. By 1998, the first indoor ProStar® system was installed at Indiana University-Purdue University in Indianapolis. Over 1,000 universities now have Daktronics scoreboards.

Now, with this new breakthrough, after nearly three decades, Daktronics was also well on its way to successes in the motor racing niche market with a major installation at the Indianapolis Motor Speedway. The company was also beginning to make inroads into another fairly new market, the traffic management display niche. Introduced that year, too, was the unique ProAd® digital advertising technology, a companion piece to ProStar®.

With a new century and seventy years bearing down on him, Kurtenbach decided to step back, pull up a chair, dream of new products and new applications for Daktronics, and keep his finger on the company's pulse as chairman of the board. He turned the day-to-day operational management over to the next obvious leader, James Morgan, who had grown up with the company. It was Morgan, as a student just out of college, who had been there in the thin beginnings and helped the company along with its first halting steps. Morgan's nimble engineering mind, creativity, and his talent for organization and leadership has his fingerprints on nearly all of the advances for which Daktronics became indisputably the world's leader. He knows the company from broom closet to its complicated fabrication machinery. It was Morgan who had taken the general concept from Kurtenbach and Coach Warren Williamson in the early years, and amongst the frozen pipes and the store-bought equipment, had built the Matside® scoreboard.

Arriving with the new century for Kurtenbach was the good news that he had been singled out for a prestigious Ernst & Young Entrepreneur of Year award. His recognition was in the Manufacturing category, one of nine different areas for selection. Honorees from a pool of nearly 4,000 nominees are judged for their vision, determination and leadership to create new industries by developing innovative business models for the ever-changing economic landscape.

Ernest & Young's national director of Entrepreneurial Services Gregory K. Erickson said that the awards recognize and honor accomplishments of outstanding men and women. "The awards indentify, salute, suppor and reward those great individuals—many of whom began with little more than a good idea and the unwavering faith that it would succeed," he said.

If entrepreneurs make things happen and if they imagine and create, than Kurtenbach's selection fit perfectly. He had for over thirty years invested his every moment and every fiber to working for the success of Daktronics.

Now, Kurtenbach, who never kept exact track of the hours he spent, or the miles he traveled or the nights and days without sleep as he worked to bring his dreams for Daktronics to fruition, was ready for a break, or at least a change of pace. He wasn't ready for the rocking chair, of course. His reputation as a leader, an innovator, a dreamer, an educator, and a man on a mission was well known. The new century held new challenges for him and for the company he and his good friend Dr. Duane Sander had built from scratch.

Plowing New Ground

It was a "double-double" for Kurtenbach and Daktronics on the warm and sunny afternoon of August 17, 2006.

First, Kurtenbach was the gracious host at a ribbon cutting ceremony to symbolically open a huge, new 110,000 square foot addition to the Daktronics manufacturing complex in Brookings. Manning scissors for the simple ceremony were South Dakota Governor Mike Rounds and other distinguished special guests.

After the ribbon cutting, Kurtenbach, Governor Rounds, South Dakota State University President Peggy Miller, Brookings Mayor Scott Munsterman, Daktronics CEO James Morgan, and others, walked across the street from the newly-opened building in the growing Daktronics Park. There, in the dry clay, Kurtenbach shifted gears to become foreman of the shovel and master of ceremonies at a traditional ground-breaking to mark the start of another addition, this an even larger facility of over 200,000 square feet of space. The Daktronics complex in East Brookings, once just a building with 14,000 square feet of manufacturing space, had now grown to over fifteen acres of covered space.

In typical Kurtenbach fashion, neither the ribbon cutting nor the ground breaking was overdone. Both took place in the rather quiet, subdued, conservative manner that is Kurtenbach himself, with no drum rolls, fireworks, marching band, fancy trappings, or long speeches of praise.

It was all low-key for such meaningful, auspicious occasions by what was now a world-leading, multi-million dollar enterprise with over 2,800 employees around the globe and with products in nearly 100 counties . But extracurricular shows just weren't a part of the Kurtenbach style. Never had been. The length of red ribbon to be cut outside the new addition was just long enough to allow scissor-cutting space for the invited dignitaries and the company's board members. For the ground breaking, Kurtenbach and co-founder Duane Sander and all of the others shared one lonely sand shovel spray-painted gold.

The austere, unpretentious events weren't because Kurtenbach and the other folks at Daktronics didn't know how to stage a glitzy, colorful show. They'd been doing that with their amazing systems, including the "big nine" that lit up that historic bit of New York City real estate known as Times Square, and with the world's largest ProStar® high definition, LED video displays for the "Godzillitron" and in Miami's Dolphin Stadium, and at other systems at arenas, stadiums, and college and school venues around the world. Daktronics has designed and installed over an acre of stunning, swirling, every-changing LEDs for the Las Vegas Sands Macau Casino in Macau, China. There is also a Daktronics video display in Shanghai, China, installed at the Shanghai Multimedia Group (SMG) building 2006. The year before, Daktronics placed one of its Pro-Star® VideoPlus displays at the Surrey County Cricket Club's Brit Oval in London.

The simple approach to opening and starting new construction on a building in Brookings, South Dakota, was a carry-over from the early days of the company fighting to survive. Then, Kurtenbach and co-founder

Dr. Aelred Kurtenbach and Dr. Duane Sander, co-founders of Daktronics, cut the ribbon making the opening in the summer of 2006 of the newest production facility at Daktronics Park. Also shown are company board members, from left, Frank Kurtenbach, James Vellenga, John Mulligan, Kurtenbach, Sander, Byron Anderson and Daktronics CEO James Morgan.

Sander were economizing and rationing their precious operating budget, and they were out beating the bushes asking their friends and neighbors to buy into their idea. They took the responsibility of spending other people's money as seriously now as then. Also, both men were products of the Great Depression and the Dust Bowl of the 1930s. They had experienced the hard

South Dakota Governor Mike Rounds and Aelred Kurtenbach at the dedication and open house of the newest, 110,000 square foot Daktronics facility in 2006, which coincided with ground breaking ceremonies for an even larger building to be ready by 2007. It will have 200,000 square feet of space.

economic times. They were certainly bold innovators, but they were also conservative stewards.

So one short length of red ribbon and one gold-painted shovel, shared by all of the dignitaries working as a team, was plenty. It was, after all, the Daktronics way.

After the ribbon-snipping and the shovel turning as cameras flashed, the dignitaries and well-wishers strolled back to the newly opened building for a short ceremony. After brief remarks by Kurtenbach and Morgan, Governor Rounds took the podium. He referred to Kurtenbach as "truly a leader in South Dakota." Governor Rounds, a graduate of South Dakota State University where Kurtenbach once taught, said the former professor's commitment to creating jobs that allow South Dakota college graduates to live, work, and raise their families in South Dakota was unsurpassed. He cited Kurtenbach's knowledge and expertise in research and said "he has proven to be a valuable tool as we work to make South Dakota a leader in research and technology." Governor Rounds called Kurtenbach a leader and a friend, "and his genuine passion for South Dakota has made a difference."

Has it ever.

And now, with the opening of another part of the huge manufacturing complex and the beginnings of another that would be even larger, Kurtenbach must have thought about where he had come from and where he had been. Opening and launching that much manufacturing horsepower was a far cry from where Kurtenbach and some of the others in the audience—including his wife Irene—had ever envisioned.

It had all started thirty-eight years ago in 1969, a little over a mile away at Duff's Tire Shop. Morgan, now the company's president and Chief Operating Officer, had been there shoulder-to-shoulder with Kurtenbach and Sander in that little 250-square-foot corner.

Next, the company moved into a little postcard-sized house on First Street, then into a larger facility near the university campus, and finally into the beginnings of Daktronics complex. The need for more space seemed never to abate. Not a year had passed by that Daktronics had not experienced growth. The company's flow charts reflected a steady climb in product, in orders placed, in square footage of space, in employee numbers, and in all other measurables—for each of the thirty-eight years since Kurtenbach and Sander embarked on their adventure.

Ironically, one of their major goals all along, that of providing a place for South Dakota students to hang their hats and set their course in life and experience real-world business situations, had by far exceeded their wildest dreams. As the new century arrived, the company's growth had outpaced the availability of labor in the immediate Brookings area. With about 19,000 residents, and a few thousand more out in the farming area surrounding it, Brookings had always been fertile ground for the labor force required at Daktronics. But now, the remarkable successes of the company required an even larger labor pool.

To reduce the troubling backlog of orders and to maintain its reputation of rapid product turn-around, Daktronics had to look elsewhere for expansion. In 2006 it opened a satellite plant in Sioux Falls, the state's largest city 45 minutes away. There, the company rented a 140,000 square foot building that had been the former Linton Manufacturing facility. And late in 2006, Daktronics purchased the Emerson Electric Company facility at Redwood Falls, MN, where the Daktronics Galaxy® message centers would be fabricated.

Daktronics' successes, and other growth of other high-tech manufacturing companies in Brookings, earned a high ranking in the number of manufacturing employees in the state. Sioux Falls, the state's largest community, employed the largest number in 2007, 13,144, according to the South Dakota Manufacturing Register. Brookings, the state's fifth largest community, ranked second, with 5,065 employees, many of whom worked for Daktronics. Rapid City, South Dakota's second largest city, was ranked third by the Manufacturing Register.

As the new century began, Daktronics for the first time was enjoying annual sales that exceeded $100 million. The advancements in light emitting diode technology and the expertise with which Daktronics engineers and technicians were incorporating the LED into its products, was impressive. Daktronics had become one of the world's largest suppliers of electronic scoreboards, computer programmable displays, large screen video displays, sound systems and control systems, and one of the largest consumer of the LED product in the world.

The company had acquired Keyfame, Inc., its animation component, and SportsLink, Inc., to handle the myriad of sporting statistics, and both further enhanced the tremendous potential of the LED technology, just in time for the Salt Lake City Winter Olympics, where the Daktronics presence was on colorful and impressive display.

To meet the needs of its expanding market, the plant in 2002 again grew in size, to a total of 368,000 square feet. During the first six months of 2003, Daktronics shipped an amazing 1,500 basketball scoreboards and 175 football scoreboards.

The company had gathered together a talented pool of engineers and technicians, and their work on custom systems was becoming legendary. Daktronics was further impressing New Yorkers and the world with a new, multi-million dollar display in Times Square for Lehman Brothers. And Daktronics was reaching out with its first overseas sales and service office in Frankfort, Germany.

In 2004, with nearly 1,500 employees, Daktronics stunned the sports world with the largest sports scoreboard in North America. That was at the Cleveland Indians Jacobs Field. The huge, $7 million board, heavily laden with a variety of electronic accoutrements, was 40 by 150 feet. That display was followed by the completion of a new, spectacular ProStar® VideoPlus®, a three-dimensional sculpted display in Times Square for Coca Cola, the successor of the previous Daktronics-built Coca Cola sign turned on in Times Square in 1991. The new display incorporated the most revolutionary, complicated, technologically difficult system ever.

Robert Madler, Daktronics' metal fabrication and manufacturing graphics supervisor in the Brookings plant, believed that second-generation Coca Cola project "took metal fabrication to a new level." He and his co-workers had to devise new manufacturing and construction processes to fabricate its curved panels. Fulfilling Coca Cola's artistic vision as expressed to Daktronics engineers by a small model of the display it provided, called for two-dimensional, curved cabinets, a first for Daktronics. If the light emitting diodes in the display were laid end-to-end, the line would be nearly 18 miles long.

Said Nate Nearman, Daktronics' lead mechanical design engineer: "Without question the Coke display is the most complex video display system in the world." It was his opinion that Daktronics was probably the only company in the world that could have completed the project under the extreme time line set by Coca Cola, while at the same time maintaining the look and feel of the original artistic sculpture. The new display was to help celebrate the 100th anniversary of both Times Square and Coca Cola Bottling Company of New York.

On July 1, 2004, as thousands of New Yorkers and tourists watched, the display was first illuminated. The video board was six stories high and its thirty-two convex and concave curved sections weighed thirty tons.

Still flush with the successful completion of the new Coca Cola sign, Daktronics in 2004 next set its sights on providing first class display and service at the Athens, Greece, Olympic Games.

The growing demands for Daktronics standard and custom scoreboards and video displays for commercial use, and the company's entry into the growing market for digital billboards and other transportation information devices added to the company's growth surge.

There was other good news, too. The company acquired Dodge Electronics, Inc., and European Timing Systems, Inc. And as if Daktronics hadn't created enough "Wow Factor" with the Coca Cola display, the Jacob's Field and Olympics creations, it placed product in the Exel Center in St. Paul, MN and the American Airlines Center in Dallas, TX. It entered the

166

professional basketball arena with one of the most sophisticated indoor displays ever, lighting up the already fantastic FedEx Forum in Memphis, TN, where the Grizzlies held court. The fully-integrated system combined multiple full-color video displays with scoring and messaging components to provide spectators with an ever-changing dynamic sequence of visuals. The center-hung scoreboard was sited to be a focal point of the system, providing fans with live videos, instant replays, and information on ten large, digital, full-color displays and four dedicated scoreboards. ProAd® digital displays provided clever, exciting animations and graphics, Grizzlies and visiting team statistics, scores and statistics from other games in the NBA, and interactive promotional messages from the team and its sponsors. Other Daktronics displays and videos surrounded the arena.

Andy Dolich, president of Grizzlies business operations, was impressed. "Simpy put," he wrote Kurtenbach, "the scoreboard in FedEx Forum will absolutely blow fans away." He said the scoreboard was the "most advanced and most impressive in any arena in the United States and will be the centerpiece of the game experience."

There were still other laurels headed Daktronics' way in 2004, compliments of the Jacksonville Jaguars professional football team, where another original ProStar®, VideoPlus® display was adding panache to the National Football League's games in Florida. Bill Prescott, senior vice-president and CFO of the Jaguars, in a letter to Kurtenbach, had this to say: "The two giant screens in the end zone, along with the other boards, are used to their full capacity. Our fans love seeing their favorite highlights and replays on the super-sized screens." By 2006, Daktronics scoreboards and video boards and other Daktronics products were in twenty-six of the thirty-one National Football League stadiums.

All of this 2004 activity just didn't happen. Research and development were key. That year, Daktronics invested over $8 million in product design and development. Even more impressive accomplishments were to come in 2005, beginning with the installation of the world's largest light emitting diode dispay, stretching nearly a quarter of a mile (1,114 feet) along the upper fascia of Dodger Stadium. And that year, the company also installed the multi-million dollar system it had devised for the Kuwait Stock Exchange.

Company product design and development in 2006 continued with an investment of nearly $12 million. Kurtenbach, now 72 and recovering from major back surgery, remained heavily involved in long-range planning as chairman of the Board of Directors. He spent much of his time helping to strategically place Daktronics on the cusp of the ever-growing transportation information field using the company's Vanguard® system. He also was giving back to the community, his state, and nation. He continued to be heavily involved and provide leadership in South Dakota's Experimental Program to Stimulate Competitive Research (EPSCoR). It was a thrill for him, still the educator (he served for a time as interim dean of the South Dakota State University College of Engineering in 2001-02), to be a part of this prestigious group of state scientists from the various colleges and universities in South Dakota, and with entrepreneurs of the state.

Kurtenbach had chaired the EPSCoR advisory committee since its incorporation in 1986. Then, with literally no federally funded research programs in the state, the program in 2006 was granted $44 million in awards from the National Science Foundation, National Institute of Health, Department of Defense, National Aeronautic and Space Administration, Department of Agriculture, and Department of Energy.

Kurtenbach was also involved in EPSCoR at the national level, helping to develop the "Vision 2020" for the National Science Foundation and increasing funding for EPSCoR. During the annual meeting of the South Dakota EPSCoR in 2006, over 150 scientists, entre-

Dr. Aelred and Irene Kurtenbach visit with Senator John Thune on the campus of South Dakota State University where in 2006 Sen. Thune announced passage of a $108 million Sun Grant Initiative at the university that was named one of the nation's five Sun Grant regional centers. Dr. Kurtenbach has always been an advocate and strong supporter of research in South Dakota and nationally.

preneurs, and economic developers attended as Governor Mike Rounds, in recognition of Kurtenbach's long service to the organization, declared the day, Sept. 26, as "Al Kurtenbach Day" in South Dakota.

That same year, Kurtenbach took time out to attend the Sales and Marketing Executives-International (SEMI) Conference in Dallas, where he was inducted into the organization's Hall of Fame. Each year, honorees are selected by an international board from its over 10,000 members around the world.

By 2006, ten percent of orders arriving at the Brookings main office were from international sales. A small manufacturing facility was operating in China in concert with Daktronics, and the company by now had sales and service offices in Canada, France, Germany, and the United Kingdom. In Malaysia, Daktronics was a forty-nine percent owner in a joint venture.

The company in 2006 also expanded its product line into theater and arena rigging systems and scoreboard hoists. It purchased Hoffend & Sons, Inc., of Victor, NY, a company that designed theater rigging systems. Daktronics had for several years been using Hoffend's rigging systems, and now, with ownership, it expected to expand the Daktronics presence in elementary, middle, and high schools as well as in theater venues, to which Daktronics was also selling outdoor marquees and displays.

When the Forbes List of the best 200 small businesses was published during the year, two South Dakota firms were listed: Daktronics and Raven Industries of Sioux Falls.

And the company was making news in the television industry. NBC unveiled a new, colorful background for its news program, "The Today Show." Four high resolution ProStar® video displays were added to the set, marking the first time the LED video display with three and four millimeter center-to-center pixel spacing was used.

In another strategic move in 2006, Daktronics joined with VST International, Inc., of San Diego, CA, to form FuelCast Media. The partnership was organized to focus on expanding both companies' reach into the growing digital media market. VST provides state-of-the-art networked media solutions to retail oil companies worldwide through the VST Media Network that is deployed through retail gas stations via fuel pump-mounted monitors that provide full-motion video and stereo sound. Plans are to make the new concept North America's largest out-of-home advertising network for petroleum products, with primary displays at gasoline pumps nationwide.

Today, Daktronics has over 2,800 employees worldwide and the company isn't resting on its past laurels so more growth is almost certain. Its already huge manufacturing plant in Brookings was expanding, and product fabrication was also underway in satellite facilities in Sioux Falls and about to begin in Redwood Falls, MN.

Under the day-to-day guidance of Kurtenbach, Daktronics has passed many milestones. They included the decision to focus on more systems oriented products and to zero in on display systems and to abandon control systems. The lamp driver circuit, or addressable driver, was an important breakthrough. The advancement of light emitting diode colors that made full-spectrum displays possible was another important step, along with the utilization by Daktronics of as much computer technology as they could find and develop, starting first with the microprocessors up to the powerful desk and laptop computers of today.

Although no longer involved in the day-to-day operations at the plant, Kurtenbach still maintains an office there, and he continues to drop in for some duties with Daktronics. His longtime secretary LaVetta Foster, has retired but still helps out on special projects.

"I'm frequently asked how we are able to keep Daktronics growing," he said. "My response is that we just continue trying to put one foot in front of the other so that we keep moving forward. We think positively and we move ahead, usually with small steps. Occasionally we have had a major breakthrough or a major project that allows us to take a slightly longer step, but mostly it's just attending to details and getting things right on a day-to-day basis. I would have to say that at Daktroncis, we've all become quite good at that."

What this quiet, modest, unassuming, thoughtful and generous to a fault gentle man has achieved in his career is remarkable. He lit up the little electronics company that would become a world-recognized leader. That's not bad for a country kid from Dimock.

Aelred Kurtenbach Interview on CNN*fn* Financial News

With Par Kiernan and Ali Velshi
Dec. 8, 2003 1:42.04 p.m.

...Daktronics, let's bring in the company's CEO and chairman.

Kurtenbacb: Thank you for having me.

Velsbi: You're going to be ringing the opening bell tomorrow at the NAS-DAQ?

Kurtenbacb: Absolutely.

Velsbi: You got anything to do with the lights over there?

Kurtenbacb: We help keep them running.

Velsbi: Excellent. You've had this remarkable growth over the years and you're ubiquitous, where are you in the competitive landscape? Do you have a lot of competition? How do you keep growing? What's changing in the world of lit-up things?

Kurtenbacb: We have competitors...different competitors in different markets, for scoreboards, business displays, for transportation, we're also a technology company and we're really an engineering company. We keep driving the market with new product introductions. Our video screens have been great. We call them ProStar@ display screens, and they've been great. They've really helped us expand our reach, our market penetration and our breadth.

Velsbi: Al, it seems like one of the tricks to growth would be to get these screens in places where traditionally they maybe weren't...outside the sports venues for businesses and maybe retailers. Is that an area you see growth in?

Kurtenbacb: Yes, we definitely see growth there. One of the strategies is to push growth in the non-sport areas. They have been growing. 1 think there's tremendous opportunity for additional growth.

Velsbi: For our viewers and investors, where are they most likely to see your stuff? Where can somebody go and say, oh, I get it?

Kurtenbacb: Sometimes Times Square is a good spot. We've got a lot of displays in Times Square, and many of the sports arenas, all the way from high schools to major NFL arenas. This fall we put new systems in for the

Philadelphia Eagles, Chicago Bears, and Green Bay Packers. We added display products in some of the other facilities around the country.

Velsbi: You mentioned high schools. It used to be a big deal if you saw a state-of-the-art bells and whistles scoreboard in a school auditorium or gym. Has the price come down significantly that most high schools can afford it now?

Kurtenbacb: The high school market is good for us. Prices continue to come down. Also, scoreboards are not really bought by school districts. They're more likely to be purchased by booster clubs, by advertisers. Some of these booster clubs have a really high income, and they have the ability to raise money. We have a service we call the Daktronics Sports Market where we help them raise money to pay for scoreboards.

Velsbi: Let's talk a little bit about the technology. What are we likely to see in the next few years? You've said there's a lot of engineering involved in what you do. Where are we going?

Kurtenbacb: The light emitting diode is a very good emitter. I think that will be the display element, but the controls is where we do a lot of work. We are able to now have much higher resolution in these displays, which require a much larger control program in order to drive all of those points of emitted light.

Velsbi: How about going back to some of the applications for retailers? I read something where drug store chains, I guess, are making use of some of these products.

Kurtenbacb: Yes, we have some national accounts that are purchasing displays, primarily for outdoors now. CBS is one; Eckerd's is another that is currently buying displays to put outside their retail facilities.

Velsbi: And these tell you what specials there are, what's on sale, that kind of thing?

Kurtenbacb: Yes, they use them to promote their specials.

Velsbi: It's a combination of going back to your existing clients, having them keep you as the supplier of these things, and getting out to new applications. What kind of growth do you expect you can maintain? You've seen this business for a long time. This is not a new technology company that's been around for five years. How do you keep that kind of growth going?

Kurtenbach: We really work on better market penetration and we think we can grow it better than fifteen percent a year top line for the next three to five years, and that means a lot of new applications to people who otherwise wouldn't be using this kind of thing. It means new applications. Also, it means expanding our existing applications. For example, in a high school, you might have a small scoreboard. We come in and put a little animation center above it so it doubles the scope of the job, and so we can go back to our customers and help them with more display products and that will...I think will be our greatest growth component in addition to adding new customers in our existing markers and then adding new applications.

Velsbi: So, add-ons, okay. In terms of retails, do you envision a world where now that some retailers have them, they're all going to have to have them?

Kurtenbach: I don't know that I'm optimistic that all will have them. They are the best form of advertising for a certain...for certain retailers, so we try to help identify those retailers and help them come to understand that it would be a good buy for them.

Velsbi: Al, good to talk to you. Thank you for being with us.

Kurtenbach: Thank you very much. 1 really appreciate it.

Velsbi: Good luck tomorrow. Al Kurrenbach is the chairman of Daktronics.

Dr. Aelred Kurtenbach and Daktronics Honors and Awards

1979

South Dakota Small Business Person of the Year

1984

United States Senate Productivity Award Runner-Up

South Dakota Engineering Society Outstanding Engineer

Appointed by South Dakota Governor William Janklow to the South Dakota Board of Regents

Elected Chairman, South Dakota Manufacturing and Processors Association

1985

Friend of Higher Education Award

South Dakota School of Mines and Technology Centennial 100 Alumni Award

1986

ABEX Achievement in Business Excellence Award from S. D. Industry and Commerce Association

1987

South Dakota Business of the Year from South Dakota Industry and Commerce Association

1988

Honorary Member, Delta Mu Delta, Dakota State University

1989

South Dakota Outstanding Vocational Education Employer

South Dakota Business of the Year from South Dakota Industry and Commerce Association

1990

South Dakota State University Distinguished Engineer Award
South Dakota Small Business Exporter of the Year

1991

Named to The Who's Who of American Business Leaders

1992

The Blue Chip Enterprise Initiative State Winner
South Dakota Hall of Fame inductee

1993

South Dakota Safety Council Outstanding Achievement Award
South Dakota Business of the Year from South Dakota Industry and
    Commerce Association

1994

Sourh Dakota Executive of the Year, University of South Dakota
South Dakotan of the Year, University of South Dakota
Entrepreneurial Success of the Year, South Dakota Industry and
    Commerce Association

2000

Ernst and Young National Entrepreneur of the Year in manufacturing
South Dakora School of Mines and Technology Outstanding Alumni
Kurtenbach family chosen as South Dakota State University's Family of the
    Year

2001

Outstanding Electrical Engineer, Purdue University

2002

Named Interim Dean, College of Engineering South Dakota State University
South Dakota State University College of Engineering Entrepreneur

2003

> Honorary member, Golden Key,International Honor Society
> South DakotaJunior Achievement Award

2004

> Small Business Administration South Dakota District Director Award
> Distinguished Achievement Award, South Dakota Newspaper Association
> Brookings County Bar Association Liberty Bell Award

2005

> Alumni Hall of Fame, Theta Tau, South Dakota School of Mines and
>   Technology

2006

> Sales and Marketing Executives-International Academy of
>   Achievement Hall of Fame
> South Dakota Governor Mike Rounds designated Sept. 26, 2006, as
>   Dr. Aelred Kurtenbach Day
> Distinguished Engineering Alumnus, Purdue University
> South Dakota Technology Business Center Certificate of Appreciation

Index

(Note: Daktronics co-founders Aelred Kurtebach and Duane Sander are mentioned frequently throughout the book and therefore are not included in this index.)

A

Aberdeen Gold Eagles, 127
Addressable Driver, 134
Al's Bar, 26
Agriculture, Department of, 168
Albanian Assembly, 112
Alberta, University of, 74
All-African Games, 153
All Sports, 122
Alltel Stadium, 83
Almhjeld, Sue, 153
Alvero Theater, 42, 43
American Airlines Center, 166
Anderson, Byron, 162
Anderson, Jim, 137
Angelo's, 62
Arnsberg, Peter, 17
Articles of Incorporation, 86
Astoria, SD, 101
Athens, 140
Atlanta, GA, 154

B

B John Deere, 7, 35, 36
Baltimore Orioles, 154
Banner, J. T. and Associates, 91
Barcelona, 140, 154
Barn, The, 115, 121
Bechtel, Friend and LuAnn, 73
Bell, Dan, 145
Bender, Don, 56
Bendix, Radar, 57
Benedictine Nuns, 18
Benson, Lyle, 128, 129

Berg, Sherwood O., 141
Berger, Brent, 117, 119, 129, 134
Bjerke, Ron, 141
Blizzard, Thanksgiving, 46
Blizzard, 1888, 10, 12
Bibby, John, 107, 129
Biloxi, 53
Bismarck, ND, 104
Bismarck, Otto, 8
Boston Tunnel, 152
Bowar, John and Christine, 48
Bowar, Lollie, 24
Bower, Lawrence and Sybilla, 14
Briggs, H. M., 87
Brookings, SD, 4, 164
Brookings Area Development Corp., 129
Brooking Industrial Development Corp., 107
Brookings School Board, 132
Brookings Waste Water Plant, 104, 105
Brown, Willie, 112
Bunny Wash Laundromat, 125, 126
Busch Stadium, 96

C

Caeser's Palace, 142
Calgary, British Columbia, 139
California Assembly, 111, 112
California National Guard, 112
Camden Yards, 154
Cardello, Jerry and Delphine, 73
Carthage, SD, 108
Catalogue Scoreboards, 151
Charlotte Bobcat Arena, 94

Cathode ray tube, 155
Chicago, Milwaukee and St. Paul RR, 15, 16
China, 169
Cheng, Alex, 133
Chrondek, 145
Clemson University, 99
Cleveland Indians, 100
Clemson, SC, 159
CNN Financial News, 5, 171
Coca Cola, 2, 93, 149, 165
College of Engineering, 68
Colorado House of Rep., 111
Colorado, University of, 72, 153
Columbus, NE, 54
Cook's Café, 115
Corner Café, 24, 145
Cotton Bowl, 140
Craig-Hallum, 158
Crothers Engineering Hall, 86
Coast to Coast, 119
Cumberland Gap, KY, 148
Customer Service Department, 104, 112
Czech Parliament, 112

D
Dahl, Faye, 101, 117, 126, 141
Daily Republic, Mitchell, 39
Dairy Science Department, 69
Dakota Boom, 8
Dakota State Bank, 123
Dakota Territory, 9, 11
Daktronics Day, 141
Daktronics Park, 129
Darrel Royal Memorial Stadium, 97
Data Time, 140
Davison County, 11
Dawson, Brad, 129
DeBoer, Joel, 90
Defense, Department of, 168
Devil's Lake, ND, 123, 132

Digital thermometer, 3, 88
Dimock, SD, 2, 3, 14, 15, 24, 41, 78
Dimock Cheese Factory, 44
Dimock, Warren, 15
Dodgers, 156
Dodge Electronics, Inc., 166
Dolich, Andy, 167
Dolphin Stadium, 80-82, 96
Dracy, Dr. Arthur, 69
Draper, SD, 64
Dobesh, Cheryl, 90
Duff's Tire Shop, 101, 102
Duff, Orville, 6, 91
Dust Bowl, 3

E
Edgewater Hotel, 142
Einspahr, Ron, 141
Electrical Enginering Department, 76, 86
Electronic Thermometer, 88
Electronic Voting Sytem, 101, 106, 109
Ellerbruch, Dr. Virgil, 86
Emberi, Fr. Tony, 71
Energy, Department of, 168
Enigma, 110
Erickson, Gregory K, 160
EPSCoR, 168
Ernst & Young, 159
Erv Huether Field, 122
Erickson, LeWayne, 86
Espeset, Paul, 117
European Timing Systems, Inc., 166
Exel Center, 166

F
FPS6 radar, 59
Falcon Plastics, 56
Farrar, Governor Frank, 107
FedEx Forum, 167
Feil, Chet, 146
First Bank & Trust, 87, 91, 103

First Federal Savings & Loan, 123, 132
First National Bank, 87, 91, 103
Fishback, Robert, 91
Fitchen, Dr. Frank, 86
Fix, Bill, Jr., 55
Fix, Bill's Shoe Shop, 42
Florida, University of, 153
Foster, LaVetta, 170
Forbes List, 169
Ford Field, 83
Ford Foundation, 72
Fowler, Duane and Teresa, 74
Frankfort, Germany, 165
Freeman, SD, Cooperative, 63
Frost Arena, 121
FuelCast Media, 169
Funke, Geroge, 26
Future Farmers of America Chap., 6, 45, 88

G
Galaxy® Message Center, 164
Garden State Parkway, 152
Gatzke, Carla Kurtenbach, 66, 70, 71
General Electric, 56, 63, 145
German, George B., 31
Gilkerson, David, 129
Gilkerson, Davis Jr., 137
Gillette Stadium, 156
Glendale, AZ, 82
Glow Cube®, 94, 143, 156
Godes, Giles, 109, 129
Godzillatron, 79, 97
Gottschalk, Oliver, 129
Grand Lisboa Hotel & Casino, 99
Granum, Ken, 124
Gray, Earl Barber Shop, 42
Grizzlies, 167
Groton (SD) High School, 121

H
Hamilton, Jack, 4

Hancock, Dr. John, 73
Hanson, Seth, 112
Heil, Bob and Margaret, 72
Highway Message Display, 148
Hitachi, Japan, 55
Hoffend and Sons, Inc., 169
Holm, Dennis, 114-115
Homestead Act, 9, 11
Horatio's, 103
Howard, SD, 76, 86
Hutchinson County 7, 12, 14, 15, 52
Hubbard Feed Store, 117

I
IDEA, 107
Initial Public Offering, 87, 158
Indianapolis, IN, 159
Indianapolis Motor Speedway, 159
Indiana-Purdue University, 158
International Roll Call, 113
Iowa City, IA, 75
Iowa House and Senate, 111

J
Jacksonville Jaguars, 167
Jacobs Field, 165
Jager, Hugh, 73
Janklow, Governor William, 141
Japan, 54
Jones, Arlo and June, 88
Jones County, SD, 64
Jones, Marlo, 146, 147
Jorenby, Howard, 112, 126-127, 137
Juel, Mayor Orin, 129

K
Koch, Mayor Ed, 145
Keyframe, Inc., 165
Kniep, Governor Richard, 129
Kock, William, 11
K-6 Air Force Base, 57

Korea, 57
Korean War, 52
Kobbau, David, 141
Kress, Jody, 77-80, 92
Kurtenbach, Alice, 22
Kurtenbach boys, 45
Kurtenbach, Carla (see Gatzke)
Kurtenbach, Denis, 22, 25, 26, 28, 29, 32, 50
Kurtenbach, DeWayne, 22, 27, 29, 46, 66
Kurtenbach, Eva, 22, 68
Kurtenbach, Frank, 22, 27, 66, 73, 89, 114, 162
Kurtenbach, Ferdinand and Christine, 7-10, 12-21
Kurtenbach, Ivan, 22, 66
Kurtenbach, Jack, 21, 25, 27, 29, 30, 35
Kurtenbach, Johan and Elizabeth, 7
Kurtenbach, John and Theodora, 8, 13, 18, 19-21, 23, 24, 40, 49, 51, 66
Kurtenbach, Lisa, 74
Kurtenbach, Magdalen, 21
Kurtenbach, Marcellina, 21
Kurtenbach, Marie, 21
Kurtenbach, Matt, 92, 138, 157
Kurtenbach, Paula, 69-71
Kurtenbach, Peter, 7, 8
Kurtenbach, Reece, 71, 73, 154
Kurtenbach, Rita, 22
Kurtenbach, Wilford, 21, 25, 66
Kuwait City, 98

L
LaSalle, IL, 75
Laber, Bud and Alice, 72
Lackland Air Force Base, 52
Lakewood Church, Houston, 153
Lake Onida, NY, 64
Lake Placid, NY, 133, 136-139
Lambertz, Jim, 129
Long, Gene, 137

Larson, Whitey, 31
LasVegas, NV, 142
Laughlin, NV, 142
Lawler, Steve, 137
Lawrence and Schiller, 89
Lawrence, Craig, 89, 90
LED, 78, 145, 154
Lehman Brothers, 2, 98
Linton Mfg. Co., 164
Lillehammer, Norway, 140, 154
Long Island, NY, 67
Lukechevitz, John, 56

M
Macao, 99
Madler, Robert, 166
Malaysia, 142, 169
Martin, Robert, 129
Matside®, 113-122
Marking, Jim, 121, 122
Mayer, Nicholas and Eva, 13, 16, 18
Mechanical Engineering Department, 91
Memphis, TN, 167
Mergenhauser, Mr. and Mrs. Jim, 72
Michigan, University of , 142
Milbank, SD, 123
Mills Construction Company, 129
Miller, Peggy, 161
Mitchell, SD, 52
Mitchell, Coach Floyd, 46
Mitsubishi, 155
Monticello, MN, 78
Morgan, James, 88, 97, 104, 106, 108, 117, 118, 129, 134, 136, 137, 138, 143, 159
Morgan Stanley, 2
Moriarty Family, 125
Mow, Bill and Margaret, 73
Mulligan, John, 162
Munsterman, Mayor Scott, 161
Murdo, SD, 62

N
Nagano, Howard, 56
Nairobi, Kenya, 153
NASDAQ, 1, 157
NASA, 168
National College of Business, 62
National Council of State Legislators, 110
National Institute of Health, 168
National Science Foundation, 72, 168
Nebrask, University of, 66, 82
NCAA Division II, 114, 121
Nearman, Nate, 166
New England Patriots, 156
New Hampshire House of Representatives,
    111
New Orlean, LA, 54
New York Islanders, 5
Newman Club, 62
Niagra Falls, 64
Nicaragua Assembly, 112
North Carolina Senate, 111
North Dakota College of Science
    and Technology, 102
Norman, OK, 159
Northern (SD) State University, 63

O
Oklahoma scoreboard, 95
Office of Securities and
    Exchange Comm., 87
Olivet, SD, 9
Omika radar site, 55
Omni, The, 140
Oregon House of Representatives, 111
Ovscheid, Germany, 7
Osaka, Japan, 55

P
Pace, Loren, 106, 111
Panosonic, 156
Parkston, SD, 3, 6, 15, 41, 42, 88

Parkston Herald Advance, 28, 39, 43
Parkston (SD) High School, 7, 61, 122
PGA Tour®, 94, 143, 144
Prescott, Bill, 167
Pollock, SD, 146
Potas, Milo, 106, 110
Prince, 27
ProAd®, 159
ProStar®, 78, 159
Puet, Walter, 25
Prunty, Mayor Roger, 129, 141
Pullman, WA, 159
Purdue University, 72, 74, 83

R
R. J. Reynolds Tobacco Company, 89
Rapid City, SD, 165
Raymond James Stadium, 83
Red Sox, 156
Redwood Falls, MN, 69, 164, 170
Regulation "A", 87
Rieb, Dr. William, 28
Robbins, Glen, 123-124
Roberts, Dr. Charles, 91
Rome, SD, 14, 15
Rooney, Andy, 80
Roosevelt, President Franklin, 24
Rounds, Governor Mike, 161, 163, 169
Russell, John, 139

S
SCR Systems, 55
Saint Aelred, 24
St. Paul, MN, 166
St. Peter and Paul Catholic Church/School,
    3, 15, 17, 19, 24, 38, 44, 47, 52, 84
Sales and Marketing Executives Interna-
tional, 169
Salt Lake City, UT, 14, 106
Samsung, 93
San Francisco, CA, 156

Sandfort, Dr. John, 91
Sardi's Restaurant, 145
Schillings Grocery Store, 42
Schlimgen, Sgt. Clement J., 52
Schlimgen, Engelbert, 11, 14, 17
Schlimgen, Laurence, 42
Schmidt, Fr. William, 38
Schmidt, Mother Jerome, 38
Schmidt, Pam, 90
Schmidt, Ron, 69, 71
Schulze, M. Bruce, 80
Schuan, Patrick, 129
Scoreboard Parts and Service, 146
Scotland, SD, 9, 16
Seattle, WA, 146
Sencore, 119
Sioux Falls, SD, 52, 164, 169
60 Minutes, 80
Sizzler®, 140
Small Business Administration, 128, 129
Solberg, Dr. Halvor, 69
Sony, 155
South Dakota Cooperative
   Extension Service, 110
South Dakota Manufacturing Register, 165
South Dakota School of Mines
   and Technology, 59, 76
South Dakota State University, 4, 6, 60, 68,
   74, 76, 79, 92, 115, 121, 122, 146, 154,
   156, 168
Southern State College, 66
Starr, SD, 15
StarBurst®, 97, 156
Star Circuits, Inc., 145, 157
Stromsmo, Keith and Betty Ann, 74
St. Louis Cardinals, 96
Speece, Wynn, 31
Sphygmomanometer, 88
Stearns, Warren, 137
SunSpot®, 156
Surry County Crickett Club, 162

Super Bowl, 80, 82, 83
Sweetwater Radar Station, 58

T
TSP, 69
Tachikawa Air Force Base, 55
Tampa Bay Buccaneers, 83
Tampa Bay Lightning, 5
Texas Longhorns, 77, 80
Texas A&M, 140
Texas Tech, 59
Texas, University of, 77-80, 97
Thune, Senator John, 168
Time and Temperature Sign, 123
Times Square, 93, 149
Tinker Air Force Base, 59
Title IX, 131
The Today Show, 169
Tramp, Sister Audrey, 38
Tripp, Judge Bartlett, 11

U
Uglum, Dr. John, 91
United Arab Emirates, 143
United Nations, 112
United States Naval Academy, 119
United States Postal Service, 115
Untereiner Brothers Implement Dealers, 36
Utah Legislature, 6, 83, 105
Utusan Pearl & Dean Causeway, 142

V
VST International, Inc., 169
VanBemmel, Al, 136
Vanguard®, 168
Vaudrey, Calvin, 91
Vellenga, James, 162
Voelzke, Vern, 97, 108, 127, 129
Vettelschloss, Germany, 7
Veniteri, Adam, 156
Venus®, 156, 159

Viborg, SD, 115
VideoPlus®, 165
Volga, SD, 117, 126
Volga Cooperative Creamery, 117, 126

W
Wahpeton, ND, 102
Wall Street Journal, 83, 105
Waltz Construction Company, 141
Walz, Verlin (Pat), 26
Watford (ND) High School, 121
Weiser, Elmer, 141
Welch, Jack, 64
Weninger, Ed, 102, 112, 117, 126, 129
Wentworth, SD, 110
Werde, Sister Marie Helene, 38
Wermers, Herb, 52
West, Art, 144
Westfield (MA) High School, 121
Wild Turkey Calling and Owl
    Hooting Contest, 122
Williamson, Warren, 61, 113, 114, 120,
    121, 159
Winter Olympics, 133, 136-140
Winston-Salem, NC, 89
Wintz, Dr. Paul, 73
WNAX, 31
Wulf, Fr. John, 18

XYZ
Yankton Freshwater Treatment Plant, 104
Yemen Parliament, 112
Yocum, Dr. Kenneth 60
Zehnpfenning, Herbert, 17
Zipper Sign, 95, 144

About the Author

Chuck Cecil was born in Wessington Springs, SD, and graduated from Rapid City High School. An aerial photographer in the Navy during the Korean War, he earned a bachelor and masters degree in journalism from South Dakota State University. Cecil is a former news editor for the *Watertown Public Opinion* and editor of the *Vermillion Plain Talk*. He joined SDSU in 1965 as development and public relations director and later served as assistant  to three SDSU presidents. He took early retirement in 1985 and built a weekly newspaper chain that eventually included the Estelline *Journal*, Volga *Tribune*, Toronto *Herald*, White *Leader*, Elkton *Record*, Dell Rapid *Tribune*, Baltic *Beacon*, Brandon Valley *Challenger, The RFD News,* and the Moody County *Enterprise* in Flandreau. He retired from the newspaper business in 2000 and now writes a weekly column for the Brookings *Register* and does other freelance writing. He has written 21 books including Pony Hills, Stubble Mulch, The RFD News, Becoming Someplace Special, Fire the Anvils, A Brookings Album, Remember The Times, Plains Talk, Myron Lee and the Caddies, Family Matters-You Can Bank On It, Going The Extra Mile—the story of the South Dakota Rural Electric Association, Nick's Hamburger Shop, The Corner, Astride the White Mule, the story of Prohibition in South Dakota, Here and Far Away, the story of Brookings County during WW II, and Postcards from South Dakota.